TEN
PRACTICES
FOR
CHOOSING
JOY

live happy

Deborah K. Heisz

and the editors of *Live Happy* magazine

HARPERELIXIR
An Imprint of HarperCollinsPublishers

HARPERELIXIR

HarperCollins books may be purchased for educational, business, or sales promotional use. For information please e-mail the Special Markets Department at SPsales@harpercollins.com.

HarperCollins website: http://www.harpercollins.com

FIRST EDITION

Designed by Janet M. Evans

Illustrations for the Foreword, Connection, Gratitude, Resilience, and Closing Happy Thoughts chapters by Susy Pilgrim Waters.

Illustrations for the Creativity, Health, Attitude, and Giving Back chapters by Marco Marella.

Illustrations for The Truth About Happiness, Meaning, Mindfulness, and Spirituality chapters by Jon Cannell.

Library of Congress Cataloging-in-Publication Data
Heisz, Deborah K., author.
   Live happy : ten practices for choosing joy / Deborah K. Heisz and the Editors of Live Happy Magazine. — First edition.
      pages cm
ISBN 978–0–06–244229–1
   1. Happiness. 2. Conduct of life. I. Live Happy (Addison, Tex.) II. Title.
   BJ1481.H525 2016
   158—dc23

                                    2015033617

16 17 18 19 20   RRD(H)   10 9 8 7 6 5 4 3 2 1

For Katie, Zach, Emma, and Quinn,
who bring joy into my life every day

CONTENTS

As the founder of *Live Happy* magazine, I'm absolutely thrilled to bring you this book. Helping people change their lives for the better has been my life's passion for over two decades, so this book is the fulfillment of a long-held dream.

Growing up, I was not always a happy camper. My dad died when I was very young. I was a C student and not very athletic, so I was neither a sports nor an academic star. I dropped out of college and went to live as a party-hearty beach bum in Florida. Then one day when I was eighteen, I was cutting grass for rich golf-club members and I took a good look at them . . . and then at myself. I now call that my "day of disgust and decision." I realized I needed to massively change my life, and to do so I began to devour personal-development books, videos, and seminars. They taught me how to improve my attitude, habits, health, and relationships.

I went back to college, then on to business school, where I rose to the top of my class. I was hired by *Fortune* 100 company Texas Instruments and climbed the ladder fast, so that by age twenty-eight, I was the manager of the Intelligent Systems Division (which was pretty crazy considering what I had been doing just ten years earlier).

I went on to use what I learned to build huge organizations around the world. My current startup has done $1 billion in sales in just four years, and was ranked No. 12 in the 2015 *Inc.* 5000 list of the fastest-growing private companies in America, as well as No. 1 in the category of consumer products and services.

I once launched a television network to showcase the leaders in personal development and produced over nine hundred shows. I did this because I had totally changed my life for the better and wanted to help others who struggled like I had. But there was a flaw in the promises made by the personal-development experts. To sell their books and seminars, they were offering what I call quantum leap promises—you know the type: become a millionaire in six months, have a perfect body in three. When the programs didn't work, people gave up on them and, far worse, gave up on themselves.

I was incredibly frustrated, so I wrote a book called *The Slight Edge*. Simply put, it's about how doing little things, and doing them over and over persistently, creates a compound effect and leads to fulfillment and success. It became a surprise bestseller, and people started writing me and telling me how I'd changed their lives. That's when the power of giving back really hit me. I got more out of hearing about others' success than I did from my own. *Way* more.

When I started learning about positive psychology and the studies on happiness, I got really excited. Here was research coming out of leading universities telling us that happiness was achievable simply by changing everyday habits. I realized that while "personal development" sounds like work, *happiness* sounds appealing. Everybody wants to be happy! And getting happier is easy to do—it's an anti-quantum-leap model. It's been proven that you can take grumpy people and, with little exercises that anybody can do, rewire how the neurons fire in the grumps' brains and turn them into more positive people. Again, small things, done over and over, were being shown to profoundly change people's lives.

Incredible research on happiness is going on all over the world, and yet nearly everyone has the wrong idea about what makes us happy. If you went to the nearest mall right now and interviewed one hundred people, ninety-nine of them would say that happiness is something that comes after you get the spouse, house, car, and job of your dreams. They'd say that the more recognition, love, success, and money you have, the happier you are.

They've got it *backward*. In fact, the happier you are, the likelier you are to have a loving marriage, to be successful, healthy, wealthy—and even to live significantly longer than grumpy folks. Most important of all, the happier you are, the more you contribute to the world . . . the more you *share* your happiness, your money, yourself. And the more you share your own fulfillment, the happier you become.

When I learned all this, I knew I had to share this knowledge with others. I started *Live Happy* magazine in 2013. As the owner, I have been privileged to be a part of the burgeoning happiness movement. I'm proud to be able to help fund the International Positive Education Network (IPEN) and to serve on its advisory board. I was thrilled to be able to speak before the United Nations on 2014's International Day of Happiness, and to be inducted into the Happiness Hall of Fame that same year.

Now my wonderful *Live Happy* team has produced this gem of a book. Besides the easy steps you can take to add joy to your life right now, it also gives you forty stories from notable and regular people who describe their journeys to happiness, to inspire you on your own. I have no doubt it will change your life. And as happiness grows, person by person, so does the hope for joy—and peace—in the world.

Jeff Olson
Founder, Live Happy LLC

*M*y six-year-old daughter, Emma, lately enjoys putting things—and people—into categories. On a recent day, while taking in a Texas Rangers baseball game, she declared that my son, Zach, was the strongest, she herself was the prettiest, my younger daughter, Quinn, the cutest, and my better half the funniest.

"What am I then?" I had to ask.

"You're the happiest!" she said, without missing a breath.

As the cofounder, COO, and editorial director of Live Happy, LLC, that was good to hear. The truth is, I've brought inner joy and my own spirited, spontaneous expression of it along with me wherever I go, for as long as I can remember. A tenacious curiosity and unquenchable thirst for learning keeps me awake and open to the unexpected, for starters. But spending time outside in nature—walking, observing, doing, and playing with my family and dogs—is where it's at for me. I am grateful for every moment of sunshine and do my best to not take any of it for granted.

What's interesting is that I'm an introvert. I'm not necessarily demonstrative, and still my daughter sees the happiness in me. She understands that happiness is felt and expressed differently by each person. Considering that I devote a good bit of my professional time and thoughts to happiness, Emma also likely connects me with what I do for a living, as does the rest of my family. When I asked my eight-year-old son what he thought I did when I went to work every day, he said, "You make people happy!"

Before I learned about positive psychology and began working with *Live Happy*'s founder, Jeff Olson, to launch the magazine, I didn't completely grasp how everyday choices in addition to the right foundation can build even greater life satisfaction and fulfillment. Doing the work I do now—and having direct connections and access to the latest research and tools—has made me a better parent, spouse, daughter, boss, and friend and has deepened my commitment to building a happier life for my family and myself. More so than ever before, I understand the importance of having a clear sense of meaning and purpose for my life—and that understanding inspired this book. I, along with the rest of the Live Happy team, want to connect you with the information and tools you need to find *your* purpose and experience the kind of joy that permeates every aspect of your life.

Our goal at *Live Happy* is to inspire people to live purpose-filled, healthy, meaningful lives and to deliver the powerful information emerging from the science of positive psychology to consumers who are hungry for the information. Live Happy is this book—and also a magazine, website, resource, and movement—about a timeless quest: living a happy life.

So how does your happiness come about? Is it part of your makeup, always present and life sustaining? Or is it like a long-distance friend or an occasional dinner companion whom you'd like to invite to join you more often but can never find the time for?

Sonja Lyubomirsky, a psychology professor at the University of California–Riverside, studied twins to determine the capacity of people to change their levels of happiness beyond genetics. Her study, published in 2005 with Kennon M. Sheldon and David Schkade, "Pursuing Happiness: The Architecture of Sustainable Change," shows that on average happiness is 50 percent genetics, 10 percent environment or life circumstances, and 40 percent up to the individual, with intentional activity offering "the best opportunities for sustainably increasing happiness."[1] Note that it's an average. For people living in a war zone or suffering abuse, profound illness, or loss, the effects of environment and life circumstances would obviously shift those percentages substantially. The important takeaway is that people can choose to take actions that will make them happier.

This book is for everyone, no matter what recipe for happiness you bring to the world. Putting together this book and each issue of *Live Happy* magazine, I've met hundreds of fascinating people. I'm so excited to be able to share their stories with you and to shout from the rooftops that happiness is a choice you make every day, that it's in your power—right now—to create a more positive future and to share that knowledge with others.

I've had the privilege of sharing meals, ideas, conversations, and interviews with some of the great minds in the field, such as Martin Seligman, recognized as the father of positive psychology, and other groundbreaking pioneers like Mihaly Csikszentmihalyi, of Claremont Graduate University and author of *Flow*, and Sonja Lyubomirsky, whose study I mentioned earlier. And I've been inspired by the work of the author, lecturer, and psychologist Ed Diener, whose twenty-five years of happiness research earned him the nickname "Dr. Happiness."

I am excited about the fact that people are continuing to drive the important research in the field, people like Kaipeng Peng, of Tsinghua University in China; James Pawelski, director of education and senior scholar at the University of Pennsylvania's Positive Psychology Center; and Barbara Fredrickson, a social and positive psychology expert at the University of North Carolina–Chapel Hill. I am especially interested in Fredrickson's insights on the power of human relationships—even those small connections we make with passersby—as a way for all of us to find meaning in unexpected ways. It also brings me joy to be deeply involved in the International Positive Education Network, expertly led by Sir Anthony Seldon and James O'Shaughnessy.

Our *Live Happy* columnists and go-to sources on the happiness front lines—including Gretchen Rubin, Shawn Achor, Michelle Gielan, Stacy Kaiser, Margaret H. Greenberg, Senia Maymin, and Drew Ramsey—are exploring amazing and inspiring topics and have agreed to share their tips and advice with our readers. In the following pages, we've included insightful research findings from the experts above, as well as personal, real-life stories that are full of promise, joy, and lessons of experience. And true to *Live Happy*'s mission to make the science of positive psychology accessible to all, this book includes easy, practical steps to raise your own happiness quotient, starting today.

You'll recognize themes of truth and redemption in the telling, such as in Celeste Peterson's story of resilience following the death of her daughter, Erin, who was murdered, along with thirty-one other students and faculty, on the Virginia Tech campus in 2007. As a parent of three young children myself, I think about her journey often. The possibility that you might not always be able to protect your children from something so horrific is a parent's worst nightmare. Yet Celeste found a way to create something good out of what happened—for others and herself—by establishing a fund in her daughter's honor and using her maternal gift to make a real difference in the lives of at-risk boys, including one who was friends with her daughter.

In 2012, the United Nations General Assembly declared March 20 as the International Day of Happiness. The purpose behind the initiative is to bring awareness to the fact "that the pursuit of happiness is a fundamental human goal" and to shine a spotlight on the need for a global approach to increase happiness and well-being.

Live Happy has been part of that initiative since the magazine's inception, leading the largest awareness campaign in North America and taking the message to more than fifty cities in the United States, Canada, and Mexico. In addition to providing giant, orange Happiness Walls at which people could share their own acts of happiness, Live Happy has encouraged people to share their happiness at work, school, home, and online through spontaneous acts of generosity that we celebrate as Happy Acts.

Monya Williams, whom you'll read about in the chapter "Giving Back," was inspired by *Live Happy*'s celebration of International Day of

Happiness in March 2014 to participate in our #HappyActs campaign. She committed to performing small, intentional act of kindness, despite her own struggles with severe illness that affected every aspect of her life. Monya took the #HappyActs challenge even further and pledged to herself that she would do at least one Happy Act every day. Her illness worsened, and a couple of months later she lost her ability to control the facial muscles that allowed her to smile. More than ever, she was intent on reaching out to help others.

After a year of *daily* acts of kindness, Monya discovered that spreading joy is a simple way to live happier, no matter what personal challenges you may be dealing with. For our #HappyActs campaign to have such a meaningful, long-term effect on one person who has, in turn, been able to touch so many others is what I most value about the work we're doing.

As the ancient Greek playwright Aeschylus put it, "Learning is ever in the freshness of its youth, even for the old." I feel blessed that learning about the emerging work of brilliant positive psychologists is part of my daily work—and that I'm able to fulfill a key part of my life's purpose by sharing exciting research and uplifting stories with you. I am hopeful that what you'll read here will inspire you to take action to magnify the happiness in your own life.

Deborah K. Heisz
Cofounder, COO, and
Editorial Director of Live Happy, LLC

THE TRUTH ABOUT HAPPINESS

*I*f only I had more money, I would be happier."

"If only I could meet my soul mate, I would be happier."

"If only I had a healthier body . . . a better sex life . . . more time to spend with my family . . . a more interesting job . . . fewer problems . . . *then* I would be happy."

If you've ever had even one of these thoughts, welcome to the human race. From time to time, *everyone* thinks about the things or circumstances that might make them feel happier. Even if you are generally satisfied with your spouse, family, career, and finances, you probably still think you could be even happier, "if only . . ." It's perfectly normal to believe that having a better life (however you define "better") would make you happier.

That line of thought, however, is also perfectly wrong.

Two decades of rigorous science have proven *beyond a shadow of a doubt* that people don't get happier when they snag that fabulous job, land that gorgeous spouse, win the lottery . . . or the Super Bowl. Sure, for a few days, even months, a sense of euphoria washes over people during good times. But sooner or later, that euphoria washes away. Circumstances and possessions, no matter how great they are, don't bring lasting happiness.

Thankfully, science doesn't leave us to wallow in our wishes for a better life. Research studies show that, although getting exactly what you've always wanted doesn't ensure happiness, *your odds for realizing your dreams improve significantly when you're happy.*

Wait. What? It sounds a little like the puzzle about whether the chicken or the egg came first. But in this case, science provides evidence to support the claim that happy people very often, seemingly effortlessly, get the very things unhappy people want. Happy people have better marriages. They get better jobs. They make more money. They're healthier. They live longer. They're less likely to get divorced and more likely to have more sex—and better sex.

If you're ready to shout, "That's not fair!" stop, breathe, and take a look at what happiness is and how the science behind it can help you live happy.

What Is Happiness?

Happiness is a broad term that means different things to different people. So before jumping in and talking about *how* to be happy, we need to define happiness—at least for the purposes of this book.

One of the biggest myths about happiness is that it's the same as moments of giddiness, glee, or elation brought on by an experience. Certainly, there's nothing wrong with indulging in activities that make you feel good in the moment. Eating chocolate, spending a day fishing at the lake, shopping, and getting a great massage are feel-good activities that have a special place in our hearts. What most people discover, however, is that the effects of pleasure are temporary, at best. Researchers have found that pleasure and fun have little to no bearing on a person's long-term happiness or sense of well-being. In fact, those experiences have diminishing returns. The first decadent bite of a cheesecake is infinitely more satisfying than the tenth. The rush you get from skydiving will never feel more exhilarating than your first jump. To achieve the same degree of pleasure, you have to continually raise the bar—and it can only go so high.

One of our primary concerns at Live Happy is to discuss happiness in a way that reflects the entire human experience. The version of happiness about which we care most is: *the human ability to thrive—to use one's skills, traits, and talents in a way that creates lasting meaning and fulfillment.* This definition of happiness is less concerned with feelings of momentary bliss and, instead, focuses more on what Martin Seligman, a leading voice in positive psychology, calls *flourishing.* In his bestselling book *Flourish,* Seligman explains that the convergence of five key components of life leads to total well-being. He identifies these components as PERMA, an acronym for positive emotion, engagement, positive relationships, meaning, and achievement.[1]

Positive emotion encompasses how you *feel* about life—both in the moment and long term. It's subjective and includes those moments of pleasure as well as your general attitude toward life.

Engagement happens when you are in a state of flow. Mihaly Csikszentmihalyi began studying flow more than forty years ago while searching for an answer to the question: What makes people happy? After interviewing people from around the world, Csikszentmihalyi identified flow—the feeling of being so intensely engaged in an activity that time seems irrelevant, work seems effortless, and nothing but the project at hand seems to matter—as being crucial to happiness. Interestingly, Seligman notes in *Flourish* that you may not *feel* much of anything, including happiness, while in a state of flow. "Thought and feeling are usually absent during the flow state, and only in retrospect do we say, 'That was fun' or 'That was wonderful.'"

Positive relationships feed one's sense of well-being and provide support and encouragement. In a study of 1,648 students at Harvard conducted by Shawn Achor, Phil Stone, and Tal Ben-Shahar, receiving social support was found to be the greatest predictor of happiness during periods of high stress. In another study, Achor discovered that people who provided social support on the job were ten times more likely to be engaged at work and 40 percent more likely to get a promotion than their less-connected peers. Relationships provide connection and can be integral to the next component in PERMA—meaning—because people often find meaning by interacting with others.

Meaning, like positive emotion and engagement, is subjectively measured by each individual. It is the belief that what you're doing matters—to yourself, others, and society at large. The feeling that your life makes a difference is deeply satisfying.

Accomplishment brings challenge to life. Trying new things, pushing yourself, stretching, and improving your abilities—simply because you want to and can—reward you with a sense of satisfaction.

These five elements comprise authentic, sustained happiness and are intrinsic to the human ability to thrive. And the good news is that you have a significant amount of influence over each of them. In short, you can determine how you experience life.

Happiness Is Good for You

Current and emerging research reveals that happiness, or a lack thereof, directly impacts almost every aspect of our lives. Perhaps the writers of the Declaration of Independence identified the pursuit of happiness as an inalienable right because they understood happiness benefits humanity physically, mentally, and emotionally.

When we are happy, we are better able and more inclined to improve others' lives, our communities, and the world. Take a look at what researchers tell us about happy people when compared with unhappy people:

Happy people tend to have stronger relationships. A 2002 study from the University of Illinois conducted by Ed Diener and Martin Seligman found that students who were happiest and showed the fewest signs of depression were those with strong ties to friends and family.[2] Happy people tend to have larger, stronger social networks, which is a key to maintaining positive emotions.

Happy people learn and innovate more easily. In one report, Barbara Fredrickson, author of *Love 2.0*, notes that when people become happier, they also become more "creative, integrative, flexible, and open to information." She found that positive emotions promoted both physical and psychological resilience.[3]

Happy people often earn more. Father-and-son researchers Ed Diener and Robert Biswas-Diener found that happy workers earn 30 percent more income than people who are dissatisfied with their lives and careers.[4]

Happy people are generally healthier. A 2007 study by the Harvard School of Public Health showed that happy people—those with enthusiasm, hope, and an engagement with life—had a lower risk of coronary heart disease.[5] Another study found that children who had a positive outlook on life at age seven showed better overall health and fewer illnesses thirty years later.[6]

Happy people tend to live longer. A long-term study of nuns conducted by researchers at the University of Kentucky found that 90 percent of the most cheerful nuns were alive at age eighty-five, while just 34 percent of their noncheerful counterparts were still alive. At age ninety-four, 54 percent of the cheerful nuns were still alive, compared to just 11 percent of the least cheerful nuns.[7] And a study by the Mayo Clinic found that optimistic people lived 19 percent longer than pessimists.[8]

Numerous studies have concluded that life gets better in every measurable way when you become happier. More important, your happiness will very likely help make the world a better place. Researchers have discovered that happy people volunteer more and are apt to get involved in social causes far more often than their less happy counterparts.[9] So if you want a better life, stop looking for things, circumstances, or other people to make you happy. *Get happy and watch what happens!* If "getting happy" sounds like an impossible task, don't worry. This book, through inspiring stories; rigorous science; and simple, doable Happy Acts, will show you exactly how.

How Can We Live Happy?

If the PERMA elements of happiness can be controlled, why don't we always *feel* happy? And how can we live happier? Those are the questions we asked when we launched *Live Happy* magazine. Our goal wasn't to help people achieve a temporary rush of giddiness; we wanted to help people understand and apply scientifically proven strategies that lead to sustainable well-being and overall life satisfaction.

The science surrounding happiness is exciting! The work being done by researchers and scientists is changing the global perception of not only what happiness means, but *how each and every person can achieve it.* Perhaps most encouraging is Lyubomirsky and her co-authors' research (cited in the introduction) that reveals, for the average person living in a first-world country, 50 percent of happiness is determined by genetics, 10 percent is determined by circumstances, and a staggering 40 percent is based on our thoughts and actions. In other words, extreme circumstances aside, people can choose to be happier by changing the way they think and respond to life. Simple acts and shifts in attitude and behaviors can effectively improve the way you experience life. But *simple* doesn't always equate to *easy;* happiness takes practice.

Ten Practices of Happiness

This book approaches happiness from the perspective that you *can* live happier every day. That said, in these pages you won't find a list of "shoulds." Nor will you read about one amazing individual who is living a masterfully constructed, happy life. Let's be honest, those kinds of books just make us feel guilty and inadequate when we can't check off all the "shoulds" or measure up to that kind of glossy perfection.

What you will find are forty real-life stories of inspiring but imperfect— in other words, *real*—people who are intentional about living happier every day. Some are people you may have heard of, but most of them aren't famous or exceptionally wealthy. A few may have touched your life without your even realizing it. Some have made huge changes—giving up busyness for a life of simplicity, starting a nonprofit organization, beginning or ending a relationship, or changing a career to pursue a lifelong dream—but most have found that well-being is often the result of small, intentional choices and shifts in thinking.

In addition to inspirational stories, we've included the science behind the wisdom each happiness practice reveals. Our goal is to inspire and equip you to engage in simple acts (or Happy Acts, as we like to call them) that support your ability to thrive and to experience a profound sense of well-being—also known as *happiness*.

And the truth is, happiness does take practice. We don't thrive by accident. Living a life that overflows with meaning and sustainable joy, one in which you look forward to each new day, requires a commitment to practice positive habits and attitudes that support and fuel your well-being.

Here's a quick overview of the ten practices of happiness you'll learn about in the chapters that follow.

Attitude: Nothing affects life more than the way you think about yourself, others, and the world around you. Your thoughts and attitude are among the very few things over which you have complete control. Choose them wisely!

Connection: Relationships open our lives to richer emotions. Science tells us that love—in a variety of forms—can help us live longer, stronger, and more fully.

Meaning: What are you passionate about? How can you make a difference in the world? What is your calling or purpose? Answering these big questions can spur you to be intentional about creating a fulfilling and happy life.

Creativity: Everyone has the potential for creativity, though its outlet may look different for each person. Creativity can spark positive emotions, improve your connection with others, and enhance the engagement necessary for sustainable happiness.

Gratitude: A thankful heart recognizes that all of life is a gift. Good can come out of even the darkest moments—you just have to look for it. Practicing gratitude can lift your spirits during difficult times and increase the joy you feel day to day.

Mindfulness: The only way to experience life is in the moment. Dwelling in the past or focusing on the future robs you of the joy available to you right now. Practicing mindfulness can help you see the world more accurately and empower you to make the most of every minute.

Health: A healthy life encompasses a wide spectrum of attitudes and attributes, including physical health, emotional well-being, a sharp mind, and an optimal measure of work-life balance. A lapse of health in any one of these areas can inhibit your long-term happiness.

Resilience: Challenges await each and every one of us. The question isn't if you'll face difficult circumstances, but how you will respond when they strike. Developing resilience can help you come back stronger and better than ever.

Spirituality: Tapping into something greater than yourself provides the perspective that life has meaning and that we are never alone. Regardless of your religious beliefs, this practice of happiness reveals why faith matters.

Giving Back: Giving back is about more than random of acts of kindness. In fact, intentional positive behavior—Happy Acts— can bring great joy to both recipient and giver.

Live Happy—For Yourself and Others

Our goal with *Live Happy* is to help you understand and experience what it means to thrive. We've been inspired and encouraged by the individuals who have so graciously shared their lives and wisdom. From reading their stories as well as the significant and exciting research we'll share with you, we hope you'll come to believe that you *can* be happier, right now. The "Get Happy!" section at the end of each chapter as well as the "Happy Acts" highlighted throughout this book will equip you with ideas and in-spiration. These simple actions will help you make positive strides toward well-being. Start by doing one a day for a week and see how Happy Acts can make a difference in your life—and in the lives of those around you.

If you're frustrated with life or are feeling weary or anxious, we hope the science and wisdom you read here will encourage you to look beyond your circumstances and choose happiness—in the moment and for a life-time. If you love your life, we hope the stories you read here will inspire you to share your positive energy and gifts—and this book—with every-one you meet.

Here's to living a very happy life.

ATTITUDE

I am the happiest man alive. I have that in me that can convert poverty to riches, adversity to prosperity, and I am more invulnerable than Achilles; fortune hath not one place to hit me.

—SIR THOMAS BROWNE, *RELIGIO MEDICI*

*Y*ou probably have at least one friend who seems happy all the time—someone you maybe think of as a "Pollyanna." If you're feeling down and need an emotional boost, this person is the one you call. We love our Pollyanna friends. But if we're honest, sometimes those friends can be a bit annoying.

For instance, when you're traveling together and *everything* has gone wrong—your flight was delayed; on the plane you got stuck next to the guy who wants to talk, when all you want to do is close your eyes; the skies opened up just as you landed in what should have been a sunny destination; and a mix-up with your hotel left you scrambling to find a bed for the night—your happy traveling companion keeps smiling. While you lament, "I'd have been better off taking a staycation at home in bed," your Pollyanna friend chatters away about "experiences to remember" and posts Instagram pics with irritatingly positive hashtags like #LifesADaringAdventureOrNothingAtAll.

The friend's sugary sweetness can seem over the top, even unrealistic at times. Still, this is the person you turn to when you're in a funk and need to find a way out; you know your friend's sunny disposition will cheer you up.

On the other side of the happiness spectrum, you probably have a friend who complains—a lot. So much, in fact, that you go out of your way to avoid "Debbie Downer," because you really don't feel like hearing about one more thing that's gone wrong in her world today. Her (or his; men can be Debbie Downers too!) perpetually negative commentary drains your energy, and you notice that when you spend too much time together, you begin to question whether there's anything worth smiling about.

You don't have to wonder if your Debbie Downer friend is unhappy. Almost every word uttered makes this person's dissatisfaction with life abundantly clear. You know you *don't* want to be like this friend. But you don't really see yourself living up to Pollyanna's optimistic standard either, which, at times, seems positive to almost to the point of naïveté. That's just not *your kind of happy*. Then again, your Pollyanna friend does seem to enjoy life much more than you and the rest of your friends. The reason? This friend has an innate understanding that a positive attitude is the foundational trait for happiness.

Your *attitude* is the way you look at life. It's a judgment you hold—consciously or subconsciously—about others, yourself, your circumstances, and the world around you. And it is the most powerful tool you can use to craft a happy life. It is, in fact, essential to your happiness. Your attitude—whether positive or negative—affects the way you experience the world. It also lays the foundation for every other happiness practice we'll discuss in this book.

Some people, like your happy hashtagging friend, instinctively view the world through rose-colored glasses and see the best life has to offer. That's because with a positive attitude life—*all of life*—seems better. But not everyone is born with an innate, positive attitude. For many people, a pessimistic outlook (which some consider a "realistic" outlook) comes more naturally and even seems prudent. You may be one who sees the pitfalls, risks, or potential downside of a situation first. If that's true, you may assume that positive-minded people live with their heads stuck in the sand, simply ignoring anything negative, but that isn't the case. Those with an optimistic outlook get hit with the same problems as anyone else, but they see opportunity where others see inconvenience.

If you're reading this book because you want to be happier, your attitude is the place to start. One of the simplest ways to develop a positive attitude is to be intentional about noticing and appreciating beauty, friendship, and acts of kindness. As you do so, you'll discover that the world looks a little brighter when it isn't clouded by pessimism.

In the pages that follow, you'll read about a few people who have chosen to view life with a positive outlook: NBC's *Today* co-host Hoda Kotb,

CEO and dream manager Mary Miller, musician and social activist Jason Mraz, and positivity seeker Susan Bender Phelps. "Chosen" is the key word. Were circumstances to dictate their happiness, well, we wouldn't be sharing their stories here. Some of these individuals haven't had particularly easy lives. Perhaps you can relate. But they all have *happy* lives, due in large part to the way they choose to see, experience, and respond to life. Their stories reveal that a positive attitude is both a choice and a trait that can be developed. Later in this chapter, we'll show you a few more ways you can improve your attitude and thereby increase your happiness.

Mary Miller

Discovering and Achieving Dreams

Most people don't grow up dreaming of becoming a janitor. But as CEO of Jancoa, a family-owned commercial cleaning-services company in Cincinnati, Mary Miller depends on having employees who are engaged, enthusiastic, and present. She's discovered that the key to dealing with the challenges of running a business, which include being able to find and keep great employees in a high-turnover industry, is to maintain a great outlook on life—and to help her staff do the same.

"I've had people ask why I'm never in a bad mood," Mary says with a bright smile. "It's not that I never have a bad day. It's just that I don't carry it around with me. We have a choice about what we think, and if we choose the positive, it makes a huge impact on the people in our lives." Her sunny outlook has helped build the family business and has boosted Mary's standing as a respected community leader, inspirational public speaker, and strategic coach. More important, her commitment to helping others see the potential for a brighter life has helped improve her employees' lives—as well as the lives of people around the world.

"What Are You Working For?"

The commercial janitorial industry has a notoriously high turnover rate, and in the mid-1990s Jancoa and its competitors faced a common problem: keeping workers. Frustrated, Mary and her husband, Tony, looked for ways to keep workers happier in hopes of slashing their high turnover rate.

"We realized people's purpose isn't just about the task they're doing. It's about what they're working for," Mary says. "What will they do with the money they earn? Is it to give their family a better life? Travel? Spend more time together? When people dream about what they will do in the future, it changes what they do today."

Based on that realization, Mary and Tony developed an innovative program to help employees identify their goals and dreams and then create a plan of action to achieve them. While employees helped Jancoa succeed, Mary and Tony worked on finding ways to make their employees' dreams come true.

That initial idea blossomed into a full-blown process now known as the Dream Manager program. Using one-on-one coaching sessions, the program helps employees identify their personal goals—whether that means running a marathon, getting a college degree, buying a home, or even starting their own business. The coaching program includes helping workers create an action plan by identifying measurable goals and implementing ways to reach them.

The Millers' unusual but successful approach caught the attention of author Michael Kelly and became the focus of his *New York Times* bestselling book *The Dream Manager*. That exposure helped introduce the concept on a wide scale, and today Dream Manager programs have been implemented by companies around the globe.

As Mary and Tony's business has grown, so has their staff of janitorial workers. Today, the company employs more than four hundred people, including a full-time dream manager, who helps keep track of the goals and action plans. The dream manager meets with employees on their first day of work, helps them identify their goals and dreams, and then creates action steps so the employees can achieve them.

Jancoa's employee turnover rate is now more than 300 percent better than the industry average, and the company hasn't had to run a help-wanted ad in years. Even better? Business is booming, thanks to their dedicated and hardworking employees. The job hasn't changed, but the attitude with which their employees approach their work has.

Mary explains that a person's attitude makes all the difference in life, regardless of the job. "Every job is so much bigger than the task you do; remembering that, every day, changes the way you approach it," she says. Focusing on the bigger picture, both with regard to the job and the dreams it helps fund, also makes it easier to let go of the daily drama in the workplace—something that makes any workplace more enjoyable.

A positive attitude, she says, adds value to life. "You can choose to make each day fun and meaningful. You may not be able to control what is going on around you, but you can choose to enjoy what you're doing and remember why you're doing it."

Beyond the Workplace

Today, Mary often speaks to business leaders and employees at other organizations about the value of identifying and following one's dreams. She notes that the principles of goal setting and maintaining a positive outlook can be applied by anyone to help improve life far beyond the workplace. She encourages community groups, church groups, and families to identify goals and commit to creating lives of greater meaning and purpose. Even if you aren't engaged in a formal Dream Manager or coaching program, she says, "you can create your own group of support and accountability." Each person in the group defines what he or she wants to accomplish, and then the group's members help one another identify steps and resources to make those things happen. The outcome, she says, is an incredible synergy.

"This is something families can do with their children around the dinner table. By asking them, 'What do you want to do?' and 'What do we need to do to move forward?' you are giving them an amazing gift. Being able to talk about your dreams and create a plan for reaching them is just so powerful."

Mary says that remembering why you're doing what you're doing can make a tremendous difference in how you respond to each day's events and challenges. It can help serve as encouragement when things don't go your way at work or in school and help you maintain a positive attitude.

"The only true control you have is in that six inches of space between your ears," she says. "We have control over which thoughts we choose to keep and what we do with them. Whether you choose to be positive or choose to be negative, it becomes a habit. You have to think about what you want the end result to be and then decide what you're going to do with what's in your head."

HAPPY ACT

Identify Your Motivation

Whatever your goal is, you're more likely to
achieve it if you know what's driving you.
Write down your reason—your *why*—and post
it where you can see it daily.

Jason Mraz

Saying Yes to Life

Jason Mraz, a singer-songwriter who has won two Grammys and sold millions of albums, is a great believer in the power of *yes*—treating life's possibilities with enthusiasm. "*Yes* is the key that unlocks potential," Jason says. "It really is the key to creativity, and that creativity doesn't happen if you say no. If you're in a theater and you're improvising with someone, if you say no, that's the end of the scene!"

By saying yes as often as possible, he's enjoyed a rewarding career and a stimulating life that includes a wide range of activities, such as performing, meditation, activism, farming, and business. Saying yes is more than a philosophical ideal for Jason; it's a cornerstone, a concept so significant that he made *Yes!* the title of his fifth album.

The album itself derived from a moment of *yes* that Jason experienced when he heard the band Raining Jane, from Los Angeles, first perform. "When I first heard Raining Jane, all I could think was, 'Yes! They're killing it. I need to work with these girls.'" That was in 2007. After that, Jason and the members of the band—guitarist Chaska Potter, percussionist Mona Tavakoli, guitarist and sitarist Becky Gebhardt, and guitarist and cellist Mal Bloomfield—met once or twice a year to write songs. Gradually, a chemistry developed. The band played on some tracks on Jason's third album and participated in a full collaboration on *Yes!* "The way I see it is, if Raining Jane hadn't said yes when I asked them to collaborate, this album would not have happened," Jason says. "If the label hadn't said yes, this album would not have happened. I see *yes* as the key that unlocks opportunity."

Beyond the Music

Jason says yes as often as possible and, as a result, has enjoyed some unexpected opportunities. His opposition to human trafficking, for example, led to an invitation to become the first Western artist to perform in Myanmar since the 1970s. Jason became involved in antitrafficking activism about four years ago after attending the Freedom Awards, an annual event held by the organization Free the Slaves, which recognizes those fighting against human exploitation. "I thought [slavery] was something that was abolished when Abraham Lincoln signed the Emancipation Proclamation, but all it did is become hidden from our view," he says. Knowing that approximately twenty-seven million people in the world are enslaved, he wanted to help support the cause of ending slavery and human trafficking in the best way he knew how. "So I signed on, lent my voice, and lent my music to the cause," he says.

Once, at a point when Jason felt he had lost his spiritual direction, someone anonymously sent him a box of books and CDs on Hinduism, Christianity, and Buddhism, which he explored. He has since made meditation and yoga part of his routine. "I use mantras to transform my thoughts from the negative to the positive," he says, "by thinking or saying, 'I won't give up,' 'I won't worry my life away,' and 'I won't hesitate no more.' That is, I believe, what makes me a positive person."

In 2006, Jason opened for the Rolling Stones at a few of their concerts. Until then, he was a smoker and confirmed junk-food devotee. But when Jason saw how the aging rockers took care of themselves, he adopted their program. Today, his diet is mostly vegan, and he takes an interest in healthy food and food-supply issues (he tries to eat foods that are locally produced). Once again, his interest led to an invitation; this time from former vice president Al Gore to join a trip to the Antarctic peninsula with scientists and activists to get a firsthand look at the damage caused by climate change near the South Pole.

Subsequently, Jason began growing avocados and other fruits and veggies on his five-and-a-half-acre ranch near San Diego. He's fascinated with urban farming, which he explains on his website is "about declaring your yard, your courtyard, or windowsill an actual farm. . . . It's the foundation for the idea 'Think globally, act locally.'" Jason's interest in organic and whole foods also prompted him to say yes to an investment opportunity with Café Gratitude, a small chain of organic vegetarian restaurants that is dedicated to sustainability.

An Open and Grateful Life

Saying yes is just a part of the positive approach Jason takes to life, an approach in which acting for others is ultimately a way of acting for oneself and expressing gratitude is really a way of understanding how richly one has been blessed. "I'm very grateful," Jason says. "My parents were always very supportive and accepting of my decision to pursue my dreams. I had always been grateful to perform just in a coffee shop. I honestly thought that my first hit, "The Remedy," was going to be a fluke and that I would return to the coffee shop." Recently, he took the time to go through old photos, reflect, and tell stories about his start. "I felt humble and grateful," he says. "I was floored that it could have happened to me."

He knows too that he never could have enjoyed such a life without the power of that one little word: *yes*.

HAPPY ACT
Just Say Yes!

If someone invites you to lunch, say yes!
If your boss offers you the chance to work
on a new, exciting project, say yes!
If a bakery is offering free samples, for heaven's sake, say yes!

Susan Bender Phelps

Taking Note of the Good

As a member of the sandwich generation, Susan Bender Phelps felt squeezed. She and her husband, like an estimated seven to ten million Americans, had been caring for their aging parents long distance until, in 2013, health concerns demanded a more hands-on approach. "I was blessed with the most wonderful mother-in-law. She was ninety-one and in declining health, so we brought her from Montana to Oregon to live near us," she explains.

Susan's life was full and challenging. As the owner of a corporate training and speaking business, the mother of four adult children, a grandmother to grandchildren spread from coast to coast, and now suddenly a full-time caregiver, she felt stretched thin. Around that time, she attended a presentation on how to reduce stress. At the end of his talk, the speaker challenged the audience members to end each day by writing down three things that went well—and to do it for five days in a row. He promised they would see a noticeable reduction in their stress levels if they could focus on the positive aspects of their lives.

Susan thought, "Why not?" and tried it. The novelty of the experience was fun, she recalls, but five days in, the process had become more difficult. One reason for the difficulty, she noticed, was her self-imposed expectation of perfection. "It's so easy to be hypercritical of your life," Susan notes. "Think about when someone compliments you on something you did. Your first response is always, 'Oh, it wasn't that great. I should have done 'X instead.'" Looking for what went right each day slowly reduced her natural self-criticism. "This practice helps you see that everything doesn't have to be a raging success—you can find happiness in the little things that go well."

After the first week, Susan felt a shift in her mind-set and decided to continue the practice every night for an entire year. She held herself accountable by posting the three things on her personal Facebook page. "The habit changed my whole perspective in the most delightful way," Susan notes. "For example, when I'd get caught in one of those Web scams and I'd call Apple support, my attitude would be 'I'm so happy they helped me fix that virus so quickly.' In the past, my attitude would have been, 'This really stinks—why me?'"

The day she learned her mother-in-law was going to need hospice care, her newly developed attitude kicked in and surprised her. Leaving the hospital parking lot that day, she got into a car accident. Rather than feeling frustrated, she recalls noticing how kind and helpful the police were, that the other driver was mad but no one was hurt, and how, instead of being angry, her husband just held her. The ability to focus on the upside of an inconvenience during an already stressful time brought her a sense of peace.

Later, when her mother-in-law passed away and her own eighty-seven-year-old mother came from New York to live with her, Susan continued her habit of writing down three things that went well each day. At the end of the year, she noticed such an improvement in her attitude and satisfaction with life that she committed to maintain the daily habit for the rest of her life.

A Habit That Changes Everything

It's been more than three years since Susan began her positivity practice, and the results have been nothing short of amazing. For example, she sleeps much better because she is no longer plagued by worry. "I have challenges like everyone, but I embrace them," she says. "I know I don't have to fix a problem all at once, and I've developed a patience that I didn't have before." Additionally, her day-to-day tasks seem more pleasurable, because she's looking for what's right. "There are days when I have my three things early in the morning. When you learn to see the positive in everything, you realize how powerful you are," she says. Looking for the good has also made Susan more aware of the world around her. "I notice the view out my window, the hummingbirds in the birdbath, and my lilies in bloom. In the past I would have rushed by all that."

No matter how difficult the day, Susan never fails to find at least three things that went well. The day her own mother passed away, exactly one year after her mother-in-law, challenged her. Still, Susan captured her positive thoughts: "I was happy that I could be with her and was holding her hand as she passed. I was happy that my family had gathered to support me. And when the transport person came to take my mother to the funeral home, she looked at my mom and exclaimed, 'She looks so good!' My mother's best friend and I did a high five. My mom would have loved knowing someone said that about her after she was dead. We were able to hug and laugh."

One of the most significant changes that stemmed from Susan's intentional pursuit of positivity is that she's exchanged her desire for balance in favor of harmony. "Balance is very hard to maintain; there is a precariousness to it," Susan explains. "But when I think of harmony, I think of music. No matter the style of music, there is always harmony. In life, circumstances will always occur around us that we must respond to, situations where we must rise to the occasion in order to deal directly with the circumstances or their consequences." By seeing her life as a great symphony in which pieces ultimately play in harmony, Susan says she doesn't feel panicked about what she can't control. As a result, she is better able to thrive even when challenges arise. "For me," Susan concludes, "this practice has led directly to happiness and satisfaction."

HAPPY ACT
Make Note of the Good Things in Your Life

What went right today?

1. _____

2. _____

3. _____

Hoda Kotb

Looking Forward

Having spent thirty years working on television news shows, Hoda Kotb has seen a wide array of life stories and events—stories filled with tragedy and sorrow as well as those filled with kindness, love, and joy. Off-screen, Hoda has also experienced ups and downs in her personal life. She has enjoyed success as a *New York Times* bestselling author who recently finished her third book, *Where We Belong*. In 2007, she battled breast cancer, undergoing a mastectomy and reconstructive surgery documented by the *Today* show, and simultaneously went through a painful divorce.

Throughout it all, Hoda says she's relied on a secret weapon to maintain an upbeat attitude and sense of humor. "The word *forward* has helped me stay positive regardless of the highs and lows of life." Hoda's outlook is genuine and grounded. "I'm not a Pollyanna; I just prefer to see the good, or at least the opportunity for good."

Instead of grimacing about getting up early for work or being stuck in the back of a cab in a New York City traffic jam, she relies on positivity fueled by forward thinking to keep negativity at bay. "When you get stuck in a rut of thinking, 'Why is this happening to me?' or 'I hate this traffic' or 'What if I didn't do that?' you're not looking ahead. You're not able to see anything good—even something slight—that's ahead of you."

A positive mind-set helps Hoda see a long day at work on the *Today* show as a gift, because it includes the chance to partake in a spontaneous duet with Carole King in the halls of the NBC studios. And even somber moments—those spent in sorrow over the loss of Frank Gifford, her co-host Kathie Lee's husband, or enduring her own breast cancer treatments—have silver linings. She says those difficult times offer her a chance to comfort a friend or to step forward and look for the good tomorrow may bring. "*Forward* gave me the strength to look past surgery and a divorce and see an opportunity to go to work and be surrounded by loving people who are more friends than coworkers. If I worked at that time in my life from a negative standpoint, I'm not sure how I would have made it through," she says. "The word *forward* is so powerful to me. It says there's another day tomorrow, so don't get stuck in the muck of today."

A Positive Reminder

The word helped her maintain her positivity throughout her cancer diagnosis and recovery. "I kept a journal, and the last word I'd write on every page was 'forward,' to remind myself that looking at what-ifs wasn't an option." That little trick helped keep Hoda from getting mired in fear about the unknown or fixated on statistics and odds. "I think anyone who has had any sort of health scare knows how easy it is to go to *that place*. Looking forward to good things like spending time with my sister, who moved in with me to help, or being greeted by a viewer on the street, who shared her own story of breast cancer, kept me from going down a dark rabbit hole."

Hoda isn't sure if we're born happy or learn by example to be positive throughout our lifetime (of course, we at *Live Happy* could tell her that both nature and nurture count!). One thing she is certain of is her mother's contribution to her positive outlook. "My mom is truly a shiny, happy, upbeat person. She wakes up and sees *forward*. She sees a new day and the opportunity to learn or experience life. Every day is a new adventure for her, whether she's going to the grocery store, as she's done dozens of times, or trying a new restaurant for the first time."

Others in her life have also shaped Hoda's outlook and help keep her moving forward. "I gravitate toward upbeat, positive people. And if there's any truth to the thinking that you're the sum total of the five people you spend the most time with, then I'm very blessed. The thing I do better than anything else in my life is pick great friends. Those connections are everything."

Hoda says her positive attitude isn't merely a stiff upper lip. "I get why there are times when all people want to do is throw their hands up in the air and say, 'No more. I can't take any more.'" Having experienced many of those moments herself, she thinks a tear-soaked pillow can, ironically, also boost perspective. "I don't believe you can 'suck it up' forever. At some point, you'll burst. So I think it's okay to acknowledge and have those moments, as long as you remember you don't have to stay in that space forever."

To avoid getting stuck in a whirlwind of negativity, Hoda thinks of others when she hits a low point. "For me, when you are on your knees and feel lost, remembering there is always someone who has it worse than you do pulls you back and helps you look forward." It isn't a matter of comparing someone's loss or pain to her own; rather, she's encouraged by the strength and resilience people show despite horrific circumstances. "There are people who have endured terribly painful experiences, like the death of a child or a World War II concentration camp, and they go on. Instead of trying to change the past or explain it away, they weave it into the tapestry of their life and move forward to make the most of today and tomorrow. That gives me the strength to see the good in my life and move on from sorrow or pain."

Hoda says not trying to erase past mistakes, heartaches, or unpleasant experiences contributes to her "glass half full" mind-set. "Sometimes there are things in life you just have to own and move forward from. They don't have to define or own you; they're just a small part of you. Once you realize that, you can look forward to the possibilities of a new day."

HAPPY ACT
Focus Forward

Shift your focus from hardship to hope. When
you're hit by a challenge—whether it's with your
health, career, or a relationship—be intentional
about focusing on what positive moments are
in store for you. Those moments don't have to be
monumental; they may be as simple as having
tea with a friend or taking a day off to celebrate
the completion of a difficult project. What is one
good thing you're looking forward to today?

The Science Behind the Wisdom
of a Positive Attitude

In her book *Love 2.0*, Barbara Fredrickson explains that the feel-good emotions that both accompany and perpetuate a positive outlook—"joy, amusement, gratitude, hope, and the like"—can enhance your life in multiple ways:

> Even though you experience positive emotions as exquisitely subtle and brief, such moments can ignite powerful forces of growth in your life. They do this first by opening you up: your outlook quite literally expands as you come under the influence of any of several positive emotions. With this momentarily broadened, more encompassing mind-set, you become more flexible, attuned to others, creative, and wise. Over time, you also become more resourceful. In fact, my research and that of others shows that positive emotions can set off upward spirals in your life, self-sustaining trajectories of growth that lift you up to become a better version of yourself.[1]

Fostering positivity as well as the benefits Fredrickson mentions is worth the effort. That said, it can indeed be an *effort,* because attitudes are often founded on emotions and previous experiences. In general, we assume that our attitudes, or mind-sets, are accurate and unchangeable.

You've likely heard about the power of a positive attitude. You may even have quotes, like Abraham Lincoln's "Most people are about as happy as they make up their minds to be," hanging in your home or office. It's true. And, as Susan Bender Phelps pointed out, when you are constantly on the lookout for what's going right—you find it and feel empowered by the presence of goodness in your life.

Even though a positive mind-set can't protect anyone from hardship or an occasional bad day, the right attitude makes it easier to cope with stress and difficulties when they arise. One study revealed that optimistic individuals maintain higher levels of subjective well-being (a.k.a. happiness) than those who are less optimistic.[2] Other studies indicate that optimists tend to be physically healthier and to recover more quickly from surgery.[3]

Where Do Attitudes Come From?

A person's attitude is shaped by a number of factors. For example, past experiences can affect your attitude toward people or things. If you had a bad encounter with a person from a different ethnic or socioeconomic class early in life, that experience may have planted in your mind a negative attitude toward that entire group. If illness was part of your childhood or took someone close to you, you may have a negative attitude toward doctors. Logically, you understand that not everyone in that group is "bad," but your gut reaction is mistrust or resentment. Similarly, if you had a car that constantly broke down, your attitude toward that vehicle would likely prevent you from considering purchasing that make or model again.

Social conditioning is another factor that affects attitude development. People raised by loving parents rather than by angry or critical parents are more likely to have an innate sense of optimism. (Studies show that critical or angry parents can alter a child's happiness level until it's set at around age sixteen.[4]) Additionally, your attitude can be conditioned by the music you listen to, the messages you read, watch, or hear in the media, and the attitudes and beliefs of the people with whom you interact.

Finally, studies show that people with positive outlooks may actually have genes that predispose them toward happiness. Research indicates that each person has a set point, or baseline, for happiness. This set point contributes to a person's overall attitude—the way he or she perceives and feels about the world. In the short term, positive circumstances, like receiving good news or a promotion, can boost feelings of happiness and cause you to feel better about yourself and the world around you—regardless of your set point. Once the newness or excitement wears off, however, you'll return to your baseline.[5]

The question is: Can you change your attitude? Can you overcome a harsh or negative upbringing? Is it possible to improve your outlook and become more optimistic? What do you do if you have a low happiness set point? Can you reasonably expect to "live happy," or should you put down this book and start working on your request for a promotion at work?

If looking on the sunny side of life doesn't come naturally to you, stop worrying. You aren't alone, and you *aren't* doomed to an unhappy life. Science has good news for you: it *is* possible to raise your happiness set point. It's also possible to change even the most ingrained attitudes. In fact, research proves that both happiness and attitude are yours by choice. You simply have to choose well . . . or positively.

How to Develop a Positive Attitude

Even if you consider yourself a realist, adopting an optimistic attitude can improve your satisfaction with life and help you thrive. But *how* can you change your attitude? After all, it's been with you most, if not all, of your adult life. The answer: practice. Optimism is like a muscle; to grow, the trait needs to be exercised.

We've identified four proven tactics that will help you begin to see the brighter side of life. By being intentional about what you allow into your mind, what you think and say, and who you choose to spend time with, you can begin to chip away at the negativity that may be preventing you from enjoying life.

Feed Your Mind Well

Media can influence people's attitudes toward various societal issues, toward one another, and even toward themselves.[6] What you read, watch, and listen to can affirm stereotypes and make you believe you should look a certain way, wear a specific brand, vote for a certain person or political party, or feed your children a particular diet.

If the information you've consumed to date has helped establish your attitude, it stands to reason that changing the input can change your attitude as well. The point isn't to limit all input, but to intentionally choose what information to consume. For example, a steady diet of talk radio brings out the pessimistic extremist in just about everyone. One UCLA study notes a correlation between clinical anxiety and aggressive radio—regardless of whether or not the listeners agreed with the content.[7] Another study found that news programs that tend to focus on negative news can not only increase viewers' worries as related to the topics featured, but also cause viewers to "catastrophize" about their personal lives.[8] Being aware of what's going on in the world is a good thing, but if you want to improve your mind-set, choose less irate and more balanced sources to get the news from. You'll still be informed, but will feel less edgy and panicked about the state of the world.

Reading and listening to positive materials is a time-tested method for not only improving your general attitude, but also increasing your knowledge and belief in yourself. Classics like *Think and Grow Rich* by Napoleon Hill and *As a Man Thinketh* by James Allen as well as newer titles such as *The Gifts of Imperfection* by Brené Brown and *The Last Lecture* by Randy Pausch, all offer an uplifting and positivity-inspiring look at life.

Improving your attitude begins when you intentionally feed your mind information that supports the mind-set you want. Pay attention to how you feel after listening to a news station or podcast or after reading a blog post or a few pages from a book. If you feel energized and upbeat, great! If, on the other hand, you feel anxious, depressed, disturbed, or hopeless, it's time to choose a more positive source.

Mind Your Thoughts

Psychologist Guy Winch notes that it is both possible and hugely beneficial to stop negative thoughts. "Studies tell us that even a two-minute distraction is sufficient to break the urge to ruminate in that moment," he says.[9] In this context, Winch uses the term "rumination" to describe the act of dwelling on negative experiences, circumstances, or worries. Though it's easy to slip into rumination, you can just as easily change the channel in your mind. Every time you catch yourself beginning to worry, stop and intentionally think about something else. The mental distraction might be something completely unrelated, such as noticing the beauty around you or remembering someone's act of kindness.

You can take this technique a step further by using mental distraction to solve or cope with the issue that's worrying you. Reframing the way you feel about the source of worry may allow you to see an opportunity to resolve the issue. For example, if you felt slighted when a coworker or friend didn't stop for a conversation the last time you saw each other, take a step back and consider reasons for the hurry. In all likelihood, that behavior had nothing to do with how the person feels about you. It may have been preoccupation with a problem at home or deep thought about a new project at work. Maybe the person was hungry or needed to visit the loo! Who knows?!

The point is, a pessimistic mind-set will automatically take a simple, harmless occurrence, blow it out of proportion, and make it all about you. Choose not to let those negative thoughts run rampant in your mind. Instead, acknowledge that many of the mind's initial worries are baseless or irrational. Then shift your thoughts and use your mental energy to think about a solution or potentially positive outcome.

Watch Your Words

In addition to minding your thoughts, being intentional in your choice of words can help improve your attitude. The reason? What you tell yourself very often becomes your truth.

When you say negative or even hurtful things, you are telling your mind what to believe. So saying "I'm so fat" or "I can't believe I'm so stupid" or "I'll never get that job" reinforces those statements as truth and creates belief barriers that can be difficult to overcome.

"Commit to not allowing unkind words about your body or yourself to enter your mind anymore," suggests licensed psychotherapist Stacy Kaiser. "If they do creep in, counteract them with something positive about yourself, such as 'I am a good person,' 'I am intelligent,' or 'I am always there if someone needs me.' You cannot have a negative thought and a positive one at the same time, so keep those positive ones coming!"

It's particularly easy to give in to self-criticism when dealing with challenges. But Carol Dweck, Stanford professor, researcher, and author of the book *Mindset,* says that one or two simple words can help your mind refocus on potential rather than failure or frustration. "Just the words 'yet' or 'not yet,' we're finding, give kids greater confidence and a path into the future that creates greater persistence."[10]

Yet. Not yet.

"How you interpret challenges, setbacks, and criticism is your choice," Dweck notes. "You can interpret them in a fixed mindset as signs that your talents or abilities are lacking. Or you can interpret them in a growth mindset as signs that you need to ramp up your strategies and effort, stretch yourself, and expand your abilities. It's up to you."[11]

Rather than berating yourself for failing to achieve a goal, remind yourself that you just haven't accomplished it *yet.* The power of *yet* is that it allows you to believe in your potential for success. It's a tiny word that could make a huge impact on your mind-set.

Keep Company with Positive People

Minding your thoughts and words is considerably easier when you surround yourself with people who know the importance of positivity. Just as bad company corrupts good character,[12] good company encourages us to be our best.

Entrepreneur and motivational speaker Jim Rohn says, "You are the average of the five people you spend the most time with." This may be true because we *already* share a few things in common, including DNA. One study notes that we naturally choose friends because of commonalities and on average may share 1 percent of our DNA with our closest friends.[13] "One percent may not sound like much to the layperson," says researcher Nicholas Christakis, "but to geneticists it is a significant number. And how remarkable: Most people don't even know who their fourth cousins are! Yet we are somehow, among a myriad of possibilities, managing to select as friends the people who resemble our kin."[14] In other words, we gravitate toward people with whom we share common traits. If you are a pessimistic person, your natural selection of friends may be reinforcing a negative outlook.

Now, we're not going to tell you to dump you BFFs in favor of new upbeat chums. We will, however, suggest that you consider expanding your circle to include people who are generally happy and optimistic. You may want to follow Jason Mraz's example and get involved with a charitable or social cause. (In a later chapter, you'll learn how helping others can improve the way you think and feel about yourself.) Or you might consider joining a club or taking a class to put yourself in the situation to meet new people. When you're there, practice watching your words; choose not to complain or gossip. Projecting a positive attitude will help you connect with people who will encourage you to be your best.

One final tip: pay attention to how your friends' posts on social media affect you. If your friends freely air their complaints or post negative or divisive comments, and you don't want to confront them about their own negative attitude, either "unfriend," stop "following," or simply opt out of getting notifications of their posts.

Your mind is where your attitude begins. Everything you choose to invite or allow inside—by watching, reading, listening, speaking, and through interactions with others—will have an effect on your mind-set. Choose wisely.

get happy

Feed your mind. Read at least ten pages of a positive, attitude-boosting book every day this week.

Mind your thoughts. Opt out of e-mail lists that deliver sensational or depressing news.

Watch your words. Go the entire day without complaining.

Keep good company. Expand your circle of positive friends by inviting a happy colleague or acquaintance to lunch.

CONNECTION

Being deeply loved by someone gives you strength,
while loving someone deeply gives you courage.

—LAO TZU

A year after glancing out of a coffee-shop window and seeing a man in a pink tank top, Liza Baritt still remembers him vividly. "This guy came along on roller skates, just singing his heart out," she told *Live Happy* contributor Melissa Balmain. They locked eyes, and Liza says, "We sort of giggled, and he waved and smiled. I felt joyful, just totally amused, completely and utterly so glad I had that moment." Then he skated on by.

Liza, a psychotherapist and yoga teacher in Brookfield, Wisconsin, hasn't seen the man since. And yet, to her, their flash of communication was right up there with many she has enjoyed with family, friends, and romantic partners. It was, in her words, "love."

"Love—like all the other positive emotions—follows the ancestral logic of *broaden and build*: those pleasant yet fleeting moments of connection that you experience with others expand your awareness in ways that accrue to create lasting and beneficial changes in your life," says Barbara Fredrickson, a leading scholar of both social and positive psychology. "Love, as I see it, is found in those moments of warmth, connection and openness to another person."[1]

Humans are social creatures. Sure, some of us like a little solitude now and then, but even introverts need to feel connected, cared for, and understood. Our DNA compels us to seek relationships that satisfy those needs.

From the most basic viewpoint, the biological need for connection may stem from the survival instinct; propagation and protection of the human species depend on the bonds of our relationships. But love and connection provide much deeper benefits than a simple response to the instinct to survive. When we experience meaningful connections with other people, life is good. Positive relationships contribute to better physical and mental health, longevity, and, yes, happiness. Without positive relationships—whether at home, within our social circles, or at work—our happiness and health suffer.

Although your closest relationships, those with your mate, children, and inner circle of friends, are most essential to your well-being and life satisfaction, feeling connected at work or in your community also contributes to happiness. You may not define your work or social connections as *love,* but when nurtured, they can stimulate a physical and emotional response that mirrors the benefits of close personal relationships. So when Fredrickson and other experts refer to the benefits of love, it's important to remember that, from a scientific standpoint, the word doesn't necessarily equate to romantic feelings. Rather, it is a commitment to investing in others' well-being—for your sake as well as theirs—and provides a sense of validation that comes from knowing that someone else in the world "gets" you.

The personal stories in this section touch on several key areas of life in which the quality of relationships is essential—marriage, family, work, and friends. And as we delve into the science that affirms why connection is important and how it contributes to your happiness, we'll also look at ways to nurture love in every area your life. When considering the famous question, "What's love got to do with it?" the answer, as far as your happiness is concerned, is *everything.*

Shawn Achor and Michelle Gielan

When Happiness Experts Fall in Love

Michelle Gielan was incredibly excited to meet Shawn Achor. A former TV reporter and anchor, Michelle had shifted her career path to pursue a master's in positive psychology. As part of her coursework, Michelle had read countless journal articles and research documents about happiness, but she believed Shawn's book, *The Happiness Advantage,* was the most applicable happiness resource for modern life. So when she needed a mentor in her new field, she e-mailed the Harvard-trained happiness expert and asked to set up a meeting for career advice.

But the prospect of sound advice wasn't the only reason she was looking forward to meeting him. "I had *definitely* looked at the back flap of the book and seen his picture," Michelle says with a laugh.

The attraction was mutual. A few short months after that first meeting, the two began dating and fell deeply in love. One year after their first date, they got engaged. They married in 2013 and a baby boy, Leo, came along in 2014.

Through their research, Shawn and Michelle knew that having healthy relationships is one of the greatest predictors of long-term happiness. In their own relationship, they've learned firsthand that, by being intentional every day about the way they interact with each other, they can strengthen their marriage and add to each other's happiness.

Positive Partnership

What does that look like, exactly? Michelle offers an example: "When we see each other for the first time after we've been away on a trip or for just a few hours, we always make sure to start our interaction by sharing something positive that's happening," she says. "Or we just stop and take a beat and really acknowledge each other in a way that starts us off in a happy, good place." Making the initial encounter a positive one sets the tone for the rest of their time together that day.

They also help each other recognize less than positive attitudes and behaviors, so they can be stopped or adjusted. "We call each other out when one of us is going down an unproductive thought path," Shawn says. "It's okay to vent, but if one of us is dwelling on a complaint, the other will just say, 'This is an unproductive thought.' And suddenly you realize that the negativity isn't going anywhere—it's just spinning you around on an emotional cycle when there's a more valuable reality you could pick in the moment."

By the same token, when either party is stressed by work, travel, or parenthood, the other asks for three good things that are happening at that instant. "Your brain stops for a second," Shawn says. "So if she asks me to do that, suddenly I'll realize, yeah, I'm traveling to give a talk on happiness that will help people. Or we're on our way to the airport for a great, fun vacation. Or I'm with the people I love." That shift in focus, he explains, moves brain activity away from the threat center, the amygdala, the part of the brain that triggers the "fight or flight" response, and creates a sense of calm.

Choosing happiness is also valuable during times of conflict, an inevitability in any relationship—even between two positivity researchers. Michelle explains that the first and most important thing to consider during disagreements is that the other person is coming from a place of love. "I know that he's got my back. So when we have a disagreement, we're disagreeing about the thing, the event, not the other person fundamentally. And we're also very big on communicating along the way, talking issues through as they pop up, so that they stay small things and don't become big things."

This isn't to say the relationship has always been stress free, although Shawn and Michelle profess that they are aligned far more often than not. Within the same short span of time, the couple dealt with pregnancy and childbirth (along with the usual sleep deprivation) and moving homes twice, all while Michelle was writing her book *Broadcasting Happiness*. When possible, they use humor as a tool to deal with minor irritations. Laughing at frustrating circumstances, they've found, helps diffuse tension.

Making Time for Love

And although they refuse to take life too seriously, they also refuse to take each other for granted. They have a rule that whenever one of them walks in the door after time away, they cannot hug or kiss their son, Leo, first. They show love to each other right away. It can be tough sometimes. "Our son is in such a cute phase, and it's unconditional love that doesn't come with any baggage. It is so easy to transfer energy and love to the child instead of the spouse," Shawn says. "One of the ways we keep the spark lit is to keep the priority for each other first. That makes us better partners." The duo makes every effort not to work on the weekends or check e-mails for more than five minutes a day on vacations. "Love of spouse can easily be replaced by love of work," Shawn says. "We love the work we do, and it can be all-consuming, so we have to make sure that we take time for each other."

Even though our relationships go hand in hand with long-term happiness, they are built and maintained moment by moment—through attention, affection, and intentional emotional presence. "The way Michelle chooses to process the world shapes the way I process the world," Shawn adds. Ensuring that the other person feels peaceful and positive adds to one's own happiness and unifies the relationship.

Constant distractions can make couples forget the very reasons they got together in the first place—the conversation, connection, mutual respect, and attraction. When it comes to blocking out those distractions, Michelle says, "Setting aside *us time* has been really, really important."

HAPPY ACT
Intentionally Connect

Commit to starting conversations
(especially after a period apart) on a positive note.

Gary and Vicki Flenniken

More to Love

For fourteen years, Gary and Vicki Flenniken lived full, mostly happy lives, as a DINK couple (double income, no kids). Without children, they were able to work long hours and reward themselves with fantastic vacations—scuba diving in exotic locations was a favorite. But even with all the fun and freedom, they felt that something was missing from their lives. They tried for years to have children. Attempting to fill the growing void, they visited orphanages, played with and mentored the kids there, and even invited a few into their home during the Christmas holidays. Those moments felt precious but fleeting. Gary and Vicki longed to hear the patter of little feet year-round.

Finally, the couple went through fertility testing, and Vicki started taking the prescribed medicine. But just three days after Vicki began fertility treatments, Gary was catching up with an old friend over the phone, when his friend confessed she was in the middle of a family crisis. In a panic, his friend explained that Child Protective Services (CPS) had removed her sister's two children—one of whom was an infant—from her home and they were now in the friend's care. That would have been fine, except Gary's friend already had four other children, including an infant. Overwhelmed, she couldn't imagine taking on two more. Gary and Vicki immediately offered to care for the baby while another couple took the older sister. Suddenly, they were parents.

"We brought her into our home with zero preparation. We didn't have bottles, a bedroom for a baby, diapers; we didn't have anything," Gary says. Anything, that is, except love to share in abundance. At first, it wasn't clear if the situation would be permanent. But that didn't stop the couple from opening their hearts and home to the child. They told their friends and family, "We don't have a clue what's going on, but we're going to love this little girl while things get figured out."

During the next two years, the Flennikens waded through the long process of adoption and continued to love the little girl, whom they knew could be taken away from them at any moment. "It was an incredibly stressful time that taught us how to pray. We understand lamentations," he says. "The joy, the *relief* that finally came when the judge said she was legally ours was overwhelming."

Ten years after welcoming their daughter, Sydney, into their lives, a phone call expanded their family once again. "We got a call from a friend who said her daughter was pregnant and in jail. She asked if we could be of any help finding a place for the baby," Gary says. After hanging up, he turned to his wife and asked, "Are you ready for a baby?" After praying about it, Gary called his friend back and told her, "We have a place for that baby right here with us."

At the couple's twenty-fifth anniversary party in August 2014, they announced to their friends and family members that they were becoming parents once again. Less than a month later, Gary and Vicki watched their son come into the world. The hospital even prepared a room for them and had Vicki snuggle the newborn on her bare chest to encourage bonding.

Concerned that the baby may have been exposed to harmful drugs while still in the womb, doctors kept the baby, Zach, in the hospital for five days to watch for withdrawal symptoms. Because of that concern, hospital staff also contacted CPS to check on the woman's other three children. A few months later, a caseworker rang the Flennikens and told them they needed a home for Zach's two older brothers, ages two and three. And a few short months after that, their older sister, Kylah, who had been living with her grandmother, joined the family.

Bonding over Laughter and Tears

In less than a year, their family grew from three to seven, and Gary and Vicki are thrilled. They know they're expanding their family much later in life than most of their friends, but Gary says, "I wouldn't trade any of it. For the first time in our life, we're looking for places where kids eat free on Tuesday nights. That's new to us." They laugh, a lot, at the adventures and misadventures that come with having a tween, a first-grader, and three toddlers, but sometimes there are tears too.

When the two- and three-year-old boys came into the family, tears were a regular part of bath time. "The two-year-old had been burned in hot water and was just traumatized when we put him in the bathtub the first time," Vicki recalls. While his older brother splashed and played in the water and tried to convince him that everything was fine, the little one screamed, "*Hot, hot! Burn, burn!*"

"For fourteen days, he just screamed at bath time, and it broke my heart. The first time he took a bath and didn't cry, it was amazing," Vicki says. "It took fourteen days for him to trust me. God makes these little people so trusting. We need to learn from that. You can start over, and life can be good again. I'm in awe of how trusting they have been with us, especially when something terribly tragic happened. Now when we say, 'Hey, it's bath time,' he's the first one running up the stairs. But even now he waits and asks, 'Hot?' When I tell him it's good, he jumps in."

Gary and Vicki expect there to be ups and downs as the children grow and bond with them, but they have enjoyed the contagious joy that has become part of their lives through adoption. "We are blessed beyond belief, and we want people to know that adopting is a way to bring joy not just to the child, but to the entire family," Gary says. "We couldn't be happier."

Occasionally, people ask if it's difficult to take someone else's children into their home. But Gary, who was adopted himself, sets them straight. "It's not someone else's child; it's now my child. God gave me this child, and this child makes my family whole."

HAPPY ACT

Hug Your Child Every Day

Hugs are scientifically proven to lower cortisol
(the stress hormone) and increase oxytocin
(the love hormone). In other words, hugging is
good for you! As children grow into teenagers,
hugs tend to become less a part of daily life.
Unlike toddlers, teens don't typically run into
your arms when you pick them up from school.
But studies show that *everyone* benefits from hugs.
No matter how old your child is, he or she needs to
feel your embrace every day.

Jenn Lim and Tony Hsieh
Happy at Work

Savvy employers today know that happy workers are good for business. They're more productive, more loyal, and make the office a more enjoyable place to work.[2] Jenn Lim, "Chief Happiness Officer" of the Zappos spin-off consulting group Delivering Happiness, was instrumental in helping Zappos founder Tony Hsieh define the company's progressive culture. She has made a career, with almost missionary zeal, of connecting the dots between happy work and happy workers. Creating an environment where employees feel respected, cared for, and connected was central to that goal.

Defining Core Values

The real emphasis on Zappos's workplace culture happened after the company moved its headquarters from San Francisco to Henderson, Nevada, in 2003. The company was growing and its customer service was unparalleled, but the culture needed some work. Tony suggested that Zappos should hire people whom existing employees might "also enjoy hanging out with after work," he recalls in his book *Delivering Happiness*.[3] Developing a strong culture became Zappos's "number-one priority." A movement was born, starting with the company's "Culture Book," spearheaded by Tony and Jenn, which was a culmination of unedited, uncensored employee ideas about the company's culture—to be shared with new hires, vendors, and anyone who was interested.

Next came the development of ten core values based on input from everyone:

1. **Deliver WOW through service**

2. **Embrace and drive change**

3. **Create fun and a little weirdness**

4. **Be adventurous, creative, and open-minded**

5. **Pursue growth and learning**

6. **Build open and honest relationships with communication**

7. **Build a positive team and family spirit**

8. **Do more with less**

9. **Be passionate and determined**

10. **Be humble**

Living up to these core values is part of an employee's job description.

A Home Away from Home

Perhaps one of the most enduring aspects of Zappos's culture—one that has defined it from the start—is its sense of connectedness. "We are more than just a team—we are a family," Tony explains in *Delivering Happiness*, where he tells how this quality is driven home by Robin P., an employee who lost her husband suddenly in 2007. Robin's first phone call conveying the news was not to a relative, but to her employer, Zappos. "That one action made me realize the strong connection I felt with my coworkers and the Zappos culture. It was essentially my home away from home." Zappos gave her the time she needed, volunteered to cater the funeral service, offered her a shoulder to cry on, and was her "refuge" and "healing place."

Jenn says Zappos is a perfect example of a company that found itself—and a cadre of dedicated, happy employees—when it realized it wasn't just selling shoes. "Zappos was delivering happiness to the world," she says. "Our model of happiness moves from the 'me' to the 'we' to the 'community.'" For Zappos's employees, that community is a fluid one, extending from work to personal lives and back again. Social engagement on campus and off is the norm; communication and mutual support are key. And, happily, so is the mandate to be "real" or your "own weird self."

"We watch out for each other," Tony says in *Delivering Happiness*, "care for each other, and go above and beyond for each other, because we believe in each other and we trust each other. We work together, but we also play together. Our bonds go far beyond the typical coworker relationships found at most companies."

A person's perceptions of friendship opportunities at work are directly related to how "engaged" that employee is.[4] "In *The Happiness Hypothesis*, author Jonathan Haidt concludes that happiness doesn't come primarily from within, but rather, *from between*," Tony says in his book. "This is one of the reasons we place so much emphasis on company culture at Zappos."

Jenn echoes this sentiment. "A sense of connectedness, that is, meaningful relationships, is one of the most sustainable forms of happiness. Over the years, I've seen our teams make choices in the best and worst of times toward connectedness. Relationships matter because people don't show up to work because they have to—but because they want to be with their friends, their tribe. And they matter because people tend to go above and beyond when they share mutual respect and trust."

HAPPY ACT
Let Coworkers Know You Appreciate Them

Only 10 percent of people say thank you to
their coworkers on a daily basis.[5] Demonstrate
your appreciation for your teammates' efforts
by saying thank you in person and via e-mail
(and, if appropriate, copy their bosses).

Judy Kirkwood and Gretchen Brant

Friends for Life's Ups and Downs

The thirty-five-year friendship between Judy Kirkwood and her best friend, Gretchen Brant, is rooted in laughter, a love of language, and unconditional acceptance—qualities that give Judy happiness like no other relationship in her life.

"When I'm in a bad mood, my son will say, 'Mom, you need to call Gretchen,'" says Judy, a Florida freelance writer. "He knows that when I call her, for the next hour all he will hear is laughing. What I get out of those conversations sustains me for months. And things Gretchen has said or written sustain me for years."

The two first met in a poetry writing class in Madison, Wisconsin, in the late 1970s, when both women were in their twenties. As they critiqued each other's work, they bonded over wine, verse, and a mutual crush on their professor. Though they lost touch for a few years, they reconnected as married mothers of young children when they, by chance, moved down the street from each other. From then on, dealing with life's challenges together kept them connected.

"In one early telling, bonding moment, I had just learned that my husband was having an affair," Judy says. "I was walking down the street, and Gretchen was walking up the street. I needed to unload this horrible news, so I told her how my life was such a wreck. She responded that she didn't have time to talk, because her life was such a wreck with both her children having separate crises. We just started laughing and never really stopped."

Unconditional Friendship

The women also connected deeply over the fact they both had family members with health issues. The freedom to be completely honest and open with each other in ways they couldn't be with others cemented their friendship. "There were days I was so drained I didn't want to do it anymore," says Judy. "Gretchen was the one person who understood and has unconditional acceptance of my family—as I do of hers."

The women's homes were also a source of comfort and refuge for each other. If Gretchen was overwhelmed, she would walk up the hill to visit Judy, who would instruct her to lie down in the "Gretchen room," a spare bedroom where Judy served her friend tea, Jell-O, or an egg-salad sandwich ("comfort food," Judy says). When Judy was overwhelmed with the chaos of her own life, she walked down the hill to Gretchen's house, where she would find clothes drying on racks all around the kitchen. "I felt so at home in a place that was messy, because Gretchen didn't care if I was messy," Judy laughs.

Later, Gretchen moved with her family to Minneapolis, and the two continued their friendship through phone calls. They also encouraged each other's creativity by sending each other poems, essays, or little scenes they wrote. Judy recalls one powerful story Gretchen sent her about how, when she was growing up, her family appeared to be wealthy and polished, but drove a car with a hole in the floor so large Gretchen could poke her entire foot through. "We are both aware of how outward appearances can mask the inner, flawed realities of life," says Judy, adding, "Encouraging each other's writing keeps us connected to our own creativity and therefore to ourselves. If you can keep that alive, you can get through the worst of times."

Through the years the women continued to support each other during life's challenges. One of Judy's sons was a teenage parent and the other struggled with substance abuse, both women lost parents, and Gretchen struggled with her elderly mother's alcoholism. "There are times I feel shame for something, but Gretchen's unconditional forgiveness allows me to forgive myself," Judy says. "Over the decades she has witnessed my mothering, and she often reminds me of my strength in never giving up on my child. That gives me strength that I otherwise would not have."

Despite the distance, their friendship provides a constant hum of true happiness for both of them. Anytime she's stressed or unhappy, Judy says, "I call Gretchen and talk, confess, complain, and laugh. She makes me feel lighter, and I know I do the same for her. That's what happiness is for me: feeling lighter. When I feel lighter, I am more balanced, more grateful, and positive, more in the moment, I feel happy and secure knowing she is my friend, that she exists in the world."

HAPPY ACT
Reconnect

Has it been a while since you last talked to an old friend? Call your friend on the phone or arrange to meet for tea or coffee this week.

The Science Behind the Wisdom
of Positive Relationships

Imagine lying on your bed, knowing that at any moment you'll pass away. Who would you want beside you holding your hand? What memories would you want to reflect on? In those precious moments, you'll likely want to tell the people closest to you how much you love them. And you'll want to be sure they *felt* loved.

Know this: leaving a legacy of love doesn't begin with words whispered from a deathbed. Love must be shared and nurtured and grown *now*—and in every possible moment between this moment and when you say your final good-byes.

We're not trying to be morbid; after all, this book is about happiness! Your happiness is actually why we're so serious about this particular topic. After reviewing the research and experiencing the joy of deep personal connections for ourselves, we want to make it clear that *relationships matter* over and above any work you can do and any possession you can acquire. In fact, positive relationships are one of the strongest predictors of life satisfaction. Feeling connected to others contributes to better health, including better immunity, faster healing, and a reduced risk of heart disease and depression.[6] In one study of nearly three hundred men over the course of seventy-five years, having meaningful relationships was identified as *the only thing that truly matters in life.*[7] The researchers noted that even when the men had money, health, and good careers, they weren't happy unless they had strong, positive relationships.

The Biology of Love

The bonds of love and friendship are integral to your well-being and happiness. "Just as your body was designed to extract oxygen from the earth's atmosphere and nutrients from the foods you ingest, your body was designed to love," says Barbara Fredrickson. "Love—like taking a deep breath, or eating an orange when you're depleted and thirsty—not only feels great but is also life-giving, an indispensable source of energy, sustenance, and health. In describing love like this, I'm not just taking poetic license, but drawing on science: new science that illuminates for the first time how love, and its absence, fundamentally alters the biochemicals in which your body is steeped."[8]

From a biological standpoint, scientific studies have revealed several ways positive emotions, including love, affect the body, brain, and in turn your relationships. Two biological responses over which you have a significant degree of control are your *vagal tone* and the release of *oxytocin*.

Oxytocin is the calming and connecting hormone. When feelings of love, connection, kindness, and trust exist between two or more people, the brain releases oxytocin into body. At the same time, production of the stress hormone cortisol is quelled, as are stress-related symptoms such as increased blood pressure and feelings of depression. This tandem event allows you to handle stressful situations, such as a conflict with your spouse or business partner, a bit more easily. What's interesting is that research indicates that your own oxytocin-boosting behavior can stimulate a release of oxytocin in other people. That's why a crying child can often be calmed by a loving parent's touch. It's also how mutual trust is fostered in both personal and business relationships. Your confidence in another person stimulates an emotional response, fed by oxytocin, which increases the person's desire to both trust you and be trustworthy.

Vagal tone is the connection between your heart and brain that allows you to control your emotions. Your vegus nerve runs from your brain stem to your heart, lungs, upper digestive tract, and a number of other internal organs. One of its many important purposes is to regulate your heartbeat. When you're stressed, the vegus nerve relays a message to the heart telling it to speed up in order to prepare the body to fight off or run away from an impending attack.

When your body is at rest, the nerve tells your heart to speed up slightly when you inhale (to quickly oxygenate the blood) and slow just a bit when you exhale. Doctors call this variation of heart rate between inhalation and exhalation your *vagal tone*. The greater the variation, the higher the vagal tone index. A higher vagal tone is associated with better physical health and mental well-being, which is why it is important to our discussion about love and relationships.

Fredrickson explains: "Mentally, [people with a high vagal tone] are better able to regulate their attention and emotions, even their behavior, and navigate interpersonal connections. By definition, then, they experience more micro-moments of love. It's as though the agility of the conduit between their brains and hearts—as reflected in their high vagal tone—allows them to be more agile, attuned, and flexible as they navigate the ups and downs of day-to-day life and social exchanges."[9]

For some time, science regarded one's vagal tone as a fixed attribute of the body. In 2010, Fredrickson released findings from a study that proved that through practices such as yoga and what Fredrickson refers to as "loving-kindness meditation," or LKM (see the next section, "Get Happy!" for more information on LKM), it is possible to increase your vagal tone and thereby your health as well as your capacity for experiencing love.[10]

Quality Matters

You may have noticed that, throughout this section, we've frequently preceded the word "relationship" with words like "meaningful," "positive," "deep," or "strong." When it comes to relationships, quality matters.

King Solomon wrote: "It is better to live in a corner of the housetop than in a house shared with a quarrelsome wife."[11] (We're certain the same wisdom applies to a quarrelsome husband.) In *The Longevity Project,* authors Howard Friedman and Leslie Martin found that data from an eight-decade study of fifteen hundred people agreed with the centuries-old proverb.[12] Studies consistently show that a good marriage—one in which each spouse feels loved and respected—contributes to both life satisfaction and longevity; it would follow that an unhappy marriage may contribute to premature mortality.

Similarly, difficult or complicated relationships with children, parents, other family members, coworkers, and friends can add stress to life rather than make it feel full and rewarding. It's easy enough to limit the time you spend with acquaintances who bring negativity into your life, but what do you do when those closest to you are the source of anxiety or stress? Those relationships are more difficult to end and—from finances to a shared history—there may be good reasons *not* to call it quits. The answer isn't to simply agree to live unhappily together, but to find ways to nurture and improve those important connections. Here are a few suggestions on how to do that.

(*Note:* There are cases when it is unhealthy, unwise, and unsafe to remain in a relationship. If you are in a relationship that puts you or others at risk of physical, mental, or emotional harm, seek professional help.)

Make Your Marriage a Priority

As Shawn Achor and Michelle Gielan noted, being intentional in your relationships is important. Unfortunately, our closest relationships are easily neglected. In marriage, people remember the promise "until death do us part," but often forget the vow to love, honor, and cherish—behaviors that make a lifetime of love (and happiness together) possible. By making your relationship a priority, you are more likely to stay connected.

Make time for your spouse. Scheduling time for just the two of you—away from the children and without allowing work to chime in—can show your mate that he or she is important to you.

Make a connection. Hold hands, kiss, and look into each other's eyes. Physical touch, both sexual and nonsexual, kindles positive bonding emotions and strengthens your relationship with your mate. Likewise, eye contact, something that is often skipped in our high-tech culture, is a powerful way to connect with people who matter to you. "When you share a smile or laugh with someone face-to-face, a discernible synchrony emerges between you, as your gestures and biochemistries, even your respective neural firings, come to mirror each other," says Barbara Fredrickson. "It's micro-moments like these, in which a wave of good feeling rolls through two brains and bodies at once, that build your capacity to empathize as well as to improve your health."[13]

Share good news. It's easy to slip into the habit of talking about a laundry list of chores and complaints. Although some of those things may be part of everyday life, sharing what's *right* with the world and each other makes your time together more enjoyable.

Give and Receive Social Support

"Strong social support correlates with an astonishing number of desirable outcomes," says Shawn Achor. And that support goes both ways—whether you're giving or receiving. A study by Julianne Holt-Lunstad, Timothy Smith, and Bradley Layton "shows that high levels of social support predict longevity as reliably as regular exercise does, and low social support is as damaging as high blood pressure."[14] Additionally, social support can improve our ability to handle stressful situations. In another study, Achor found that people who provided social support at work were ten times more likely to be engaged in their work and 40 percent more likely to get a promotion than their coworkers who kept to themselves.[15]

Dan Buettner, author of *The Blue Zones,* explains that people in the "blue zones"—geographic areas with the highest concentration of people age one hundred or older—care about one another. They look out for one another. They worry about one another. And over the years, these deep and numerous relationships foster a sense of connectedness that leads to increased happiness, a known precursor to longevity.[16]

The ability to give support—to be there for people during hard times—and the willingness to lean on friends and family members when you hit a rough patch can strengthen your relationships.

Have Fun with Others

When was the last time you laughed with a friend until tears rolled down your cheeks? Have you played on the floor recently with your little ones or hung out with your teenagers doing something they enjoy? How long has it been since you've spent a weekend away with your spouse—just the two of you?

Sharing positive experiences nurtures relationships in a number of ways. One study, for example, noted, "Partners who are motivated to engage in fun and exciting activities together, such as outdoor sports and travel, also tend to have high levels of marital satisfaction."[17] And if you've spent any time laughing with your coworkers, you know that laughter not only releases tension and lightens the mood; it's often part of great memories. Another study even found that "closeness between strangers was increased through a shared humorous experience."[18]

Spend Time with Those Who Matter Most

Relationships—especially with our family and friends—are one of the largest pillars upon which our happiness is built. And when we foster them, when we invest ourselves and our time, we receive the ultimate gifts: love and long-lasting happiness.

But the connection between love, happiness, and relationships isn't a one-way street; it's actually quite the opposite. As the experts have explained here, when we feel loved and are happy, our relationships tend to be more fulfilling, and our happiness becomes contagious.

So take time out for the people who matter most to you. Deepen your existing relationships and be open to forming new connections—it's the best decision you'll ever make.

get happy

Trade technology for touch (at least temporarily). When you really want to connect, hold your partner's hands, look your coworker in the eyes, hug your child. Eye contact and physical touch increase connection.

Try a loving-kindness meditation (LKM). Visit Barbara Fredrickson's site (positivityresonance.com/meditations.html) for a guided loving-kindness meditation.

Ask, "How can I help?" Remember that relationships are more important than whatever's keeping you busy. When you see a friend or coworker struggling, ask how you can help.

Ask, "Can you help me?" One key benefit of relationships is that you don't have to do life alone. Allowing others to help you not only lightens your load, but also strengthens the bonds between friends.

MEANING

There is not one big cosmic meaning for all;
there is only the meaning we each give to our life,
an individual meaning, an individual plot,
like an individual novel, a book for each person.

—ANAÏS NIN

What is the meaning of life?

That age-old question has been personalized and rephrased countless ways. "How can I make my life matter?" "Why am I here?" "What's my calling?" "How can I find purpose?" "How can I make a difference?" "Does my life mean anything?" "What legacy will I leave?"

The craving that compels such questions is our desire to know how we fit into the world's grander scheme. We want our lives to matter. It makes sense, then, that when Martin Seligman defines the five traits that contribute to authentic and sustained happiness, *meaning* is on the list.

The trouble with a word like "meaning" is that it is often used interchangeably with the word "purpose." But purpose and meaning aren't the same. *Purpose* comes from fulfilling the human need to do something with your life. *Meaning* is derived from the sense of significance that comes from your purpose. The distinction between these two words is important, because knowing (or discovering) your purpose can help you find meaning.

Psychologist Michael Steger, a leading researcher and expert on meaning, explains that having a sense of meaning in life is critical to your well-being. "People who feel this way, who have a sense of meaning in life, also report feeling more happy, more satisfied with their lives, less depressed and anxious, and more satisfied with their jobs."[1] Steger notes that it may even be a life-or-death matter. He points to one study concerning longevity in older adults that provides clear evidence of the human need for meaning. Researcher Patricia Boyle and her colleagues at Rush University Medical Center found that elderly people who felt that their lives were rich in meaning had a *57 percent less hazard of dying* during the five-year study when compared to those who believed their lives had no meaning.[2]

In other words, those who have a strong sense of meaning, who feel that their life matters, tend to live long, happy lives.

In the personal stories that follow, you'll read about people who each have a clear purpose from which they derive meaning. You'll notice that, although their careers vary, each one's purpose shares a common theme of service; helping, entertaining, encouraging, or coaching others brings significance to their lives. In fact, service—whether to clients, employees, friends, family members, or the planet—may well be the key to discovering how *you* fit into the world and what will give your life meaning. One of the truths about meaning is that it is difficult to find or create in your life if your only aim is to serve yourself. Relationships and social connection—whether personal or professional—are important, if not essential, to finding one's meaning. As you read these stories, think about your own skills, talents, knowledge and how these things could benefit others.

Alastair Moock

Performing a Service

With his gravelly, old-timey voice, singer-songwriter Alastair Moock had made a name for himself singing Woody Guthrie tunes and his own compositions about modern-day "folks." Despite international acclaim and many awards, however, he still felt something was missing from his music and his life.

Alastair admits it "takes a certain kind of delusion to make a career in the arts." Earning a living as a musician was a challenge, but when it came to a career, "Nothing other than music felt fulfilling at all," he says. His other passion was working with children, but he was afraid to combine the two. "I had always kept them separate for a reason. I knew they were going to come together, and I was not ready, because I did not want to be a 'children's performer.'"

Although he appreciated the talents of musical heroes like Pete Seeger and Leadbelly, who had successfully produced music for children as well as adults, Alastair explains, "I wanted to establish myself as a professional musician and *then* make a kids' album." So he kept his two passions separate. He focused more on music for adults and filled his spare time working with kids in after-school programs and teaching private lessons to younger musicians.

Giving In to the Muse

Shortly before his wife gave birth to twins, however, Alastair began to look at his life and art differently. He needed to earn more money to support his growing family. He saw that many of his colleagues and mentors, like Shel Silverstein and Dan Zanes, weren't pigeonholed as "kids' performers." "They just liked writing songs for people and realized that kids are people too." With that realization, he dared to combine his passions and release the family-friendly album *A Cow Says Moock* in 2009 and *These Are My Friends* in 2011.

"It ended up being far more successful than anything I had ever done before," he says with a laugh. "It felt essential in a way that nothing I had ever done did. It felt as if I was serving a purpose in the world, and I felt very good about that."

After the release of *Friends,* Alastair's audiences began to grow not only in size but also in demographic range. "It was the first time that parents were telling me their kids were wearing out an album by any artist," he recalls.

Having discovered (or finally given into) his true muse, Alastair felt that he was on a good path. That is, until his path took a tragic turn. About two years after *Friends* came out, one of Alastair's twins was diagnosed with cancer. "It turned everything upside down," he says. "Life stopped."

Music Therapy

Although he had far more on his mind than music, Alastair found that playing his guitar in his daughter's hospital room helped them both get through a very trying period. "It was the last thing I felt like doing," he admits, "but it felt essential because it was serving a function."

His daughter sang along with him. Their daily duets led to their co-writing new songs that ended up on a new album. *Singing Our Way Through* eventually garnered him a number of TV appearances, a 2013 *People* magazine Best Kids' Album Pick, and a Grammy nomination.

"It was therapeutic for both of us," Alastair says. And it ended up helping others as well. The album was used to raise funds and awareness for other illnesses and families in need of support, and the lyrics resonated with families who were facing health crises of their own. "We were dealing with these issues that all families struggling with [illness] have to deal with," Alastair explains when asked why he feels the album was so widely accepted and embraced. "The songs just came, and they felt useful. It felt like my entire life was preparing for this moment."

In addition to connecting to more audiences, Alastair feels the album helped reconnect him to his art. "It reconnected me to music in a way that I had lost over twenty years of a professional career," he observes. Alastair is sure that both his musical journey and his life have been forever changed by the disease that affected every member of his family. "I guess there's nothing like writing music about cancer to sharpen your focus," he says.

Grateful for the opportunity to serve through his art, he says, "The goal is to put something in the world that feels meaningful."

HAPPY ACT

Use Your Unique Gifts to Encourage Someone Today!

What can you put out into the world that could make someone smile? It might be a song, a short video, a blog post, or even a book that shares your story.

Kerry Stallo

Jumping Off the Career Track

Life is short. Kerry Stallo first learned that lesson at fourteen when her dad died of cancer. She learned it again at thirty-six, when her sister died of cancer, and then again at forty-two, when her mom died of congestive heart failure. But it wasn't until that final loss that Kerry realized she had to make some dramatic changes in her life.

Kerry had always been successful. She ran track, played volleyball and softball, and was a straight-A student, scoring high enough on advanced-placement tests to skip almost an entire year of classes at Virginia Tech. She was fascinated by biology, health, and fitness and thought about a career in medicine. But becoming a doctor would take longer than she wanted—she was not interested in another four years of school after completing her undergraduate degree. "It was the early 1980s and everybody was going to business school, so I thought [studying business was] what I needed to do." Kerry majored in economics.

After college, she quickly secured a steady succession of great jobs in fashion retail and wholesale. Soon she was earning a six-figure salary and receiving raises, bonuses, promotions, and prestigious awards at the company where she worked. She was on track for upper management—but that's what it was: a track, going one way, with no slowing down.

And no exit, or so it seemed. When she was in her thirties, the corporation that employed her went through a restructuring and her job description changed. Dissatisfied with the revised role, Kerry resigned, went into business for herself as a consultant, and ended up earning more money than she made working full-time. She also went through a divorce around this time, which, along with the career change, led to revelations: "I didn't have to settle or just be satisfied, and I was the only one who could make me happy."

Still, she didn't have everything figured out. For a little more stability, she moved back into the corporate world. But nothing really changed except the name on her paycheck. The work grew increasingly demanding, every sales goal had to be topped, and every day was a work day, even on vacations.

Meanwhile her mother's health was declining. Following two major strokes, she spent time in rehabilitation facilities. While visiting her there, Kerry met several patients who had suffered heart attacks or serious issues related to diabetes. Though many of these patients were younger than her mother, they seemed resigned to having poor health for the rest of their lives. "I thought, 'Someone needs to do something to help people to realize advancing age does not have to equal disease,'" she remembers.

A Call to Action

Her mom lived an extremely active life through five open-heart surgeries, strokes, and cancer. As a widow with two kids still at home, she went to college to study nutrition. She took gourmet cooking classes, gardened, and did volunteer work and aerobics. Her death was a call to action for Kerry—but to do what?

"I continued going to work," Kerry says, "and every day I would say, 'I'm selling handbags. I'm just selling handbags.'"

She noticed older colleagues growing increasingly unhealthy from overwork, poor diets, and sedentary lifestyles. Then, even though Kerry was cycling regularly, going to the gym, and doing yoga, her health began to suffer; she got reflux and shortness of breath. "I thought, 'Wait a minute, I'm a really healthy person. What's wrong with this picture?' That's when I really decided that I needed to do something different. So I just drew on my passion. What did I love?"

Kerry knew she wanted to work with older adults to help prevent disease, but there was no business model for that at that time. Younger adults remained the target market for fitness centers.

Confident that she'd figure it out, Kerry spent her spare time pursuing certifications to work as a personal trainer and teach older adults how to exercise safely. And she padded her savings, so she could survive for a few months without an income when the time came to launch her new venture.

At work, her staff was down by two people, so Kerry was doing the work of three. She pleaded unsuccessfully with her managers to hire help. She tried to resign, and the company gave her an immediate raise, a bonus, and a signed promise to hire her help. But help was not forthcoming. So in early 2008, she quit, ending a twenty-seven-year career.

"It was at that time that I realized the money didn't matter," she says. "In the back of my mind I knew that I would never last another twenty years doing something that was sort of meaningless."

Kerry used her sales skills to persuade a local senior center of the need for fitness classes. She still teaches there today and at other centers. She's working on a book and a video. She's picked up numerous clients, some who have become lifelong friends. She's worked with dementia patients, people with injuries, and clients who had never gone to a gym before.

Today, Kerry spends her spare time learning about ways to motivate people. She's seen clients achieve goals and regain stamina, balance, and energy. Like the woman who climbed a ladder for the first time in years without the fear of losing her balance. And the former competitive swimmer, battered after years of hard training, who recovered from her injuries and is setting records for her age group. And the woman who had double hip replacements and worked for six months just to lift her foot to tie her shoe.

"Do you know how much happiness that brought her?" Kerry says. "Every day when I leave work, I'm satisfied that I've done my best. I've helped change people's vision of themselves and what they're capable of doing, and in some cases I might've even helped save lives."

HAPPY ACT
Pay Attention!

If you're feeling stuck, wondering what your purpose could be or how you could create a life with more meaning, start by paying attention to what's going on around you. Over the next few days, make a list of needs you notice in your community. Then review your list and see if you have a skill or expertise that could fill one or more of those needs.

Rebecca Weiss

Delivering Cheer

Every day, Rebecca Weiss looks at a little frame on her desk and is reminded why she started a nonprofit that sends postmastectomy care packages to women across the nation. Inside the frame, Scrabble tiles spell out the name of her nonprofit, Bob's Boxes. The framed tiles were a gift from a grateful recipient of one of Rebecca's packages. But what the woman who sent the gift couldn't have realized was the special connection for Rebecca between Scrabble and her late father—a Scrabble champ and the namesake of Bob's Boxes. "That gift felt like some sort of message from him," she says. Perhaps the message is simply that what she does matters.

A Sudden Shift in Focus

A couple of years ago, Rebecca purchased items similar to those she now puts in her care packages—not for a friend or family member, but for herself. She was a forty-three-year-old working mom who, like many women, felt overwhelmed by the day-to-day challenges of managing a career and a busy family. Then, in February 2014, she was diagnosed with stage III breast cancer.

"Learning that you have a life-threatening illness takes you out of your everyday thoughts," she says. In an instant, she knew she had to get a grip. "I got over myself when I learned the cancer had spread to my lymph nodes, that I'd lose both breasts, that I'd have to do a full course of chemo, which would make my hair fall out, and I'd have to do radiation," Rebecca says.

Despite the disparaging news, Rebecca was keenly aware of the support that surrounded her. "My husband, Mike, was with me every step of the way, while making sure our two kids were all set too," Rebecca recalls. Her parents made weekly, 250-mile treks to her home to help with the children, go to the grocery store, and make life feel as normal as possible. Rebecca powered through eight rounds of chemo in sixteen weeks, and her dad was there for every infusion. And her parents' practical help and calm presence soothed her as she recovered from a double mastectomy in October 2014.

"A surgery like that will show you what you're made of," Rebecca says. "It's unbelievably painful. There are so many muscles between shoulders and abs that help you sit up, lie down, breathe. After the surgery, these muscles screamed in agony. I also had to look in the mirror and see that my breasts were gone. I had many rough days coming to terms with that."

Inspired to Help

About three weeks postop, Rebecca felt well enough to hit a neighborhood tag sale, where she met Danielle, who was worried about her own upcoming mastectomy. Rebecca understood Danielle's fears all too well and wanted to do something nice for her. "I got her some things I needed after my surgery, like button-front pj's and a cute pillow that fit under her arm to support it after surgery." She dropped off the care package, and a few weeks later a grateful Danielle sent a picture of herself with the pillow.

From November to January, Rebecca underwent radiation treatments five days a week for six weeks. During that same time, she learned that her father had a mass in his brain. Her final radiation treatment was on January 2, 2015. But even though she considered herself to be cancer-free, she says, "It wasn't time to celebrate, because my dad was getting progressively worse."

When Bob passed away a month later, Rebecca's deep grief was eased by the countless stories his coworkers and friends shared of her dad's kindness and thoughtfulness. She wanted to honor her father's legacy with a donation to a charity, but had a hard time deciding which one to choose, until she read the funeral notice her mom submitted to the local paper. Her mother asked people to send a donation in Bob's honor to Johns Hopkins, where he was treated, or a breast-cancer charity of their choice in lieu of flowers. Something clicked for Rebecca.

"Maybe we could send out some care packages to cancer patients like we did for Danielle? Maybe start with the money that we would have put toward a donation?" she told her husband. Mike said, "Do it, and call it Bob's Boxes." When she bounced the idea off her brother the next day he said, "Yes, do that. Call it Bob's Boxes." She took the fact that her husband and brother had independently come up with the same name as a sign and launched the nonprofit. Within a few weeks, Bob's Boxes had raised $1,000 and sent out ten boxes. And the requests for care packages keep coming.

"It feels so good to honor him. My hope is that we get funding or a grant that enables us to give a box to every mastectomy patient who comes through a cancer center or hospital," Rebecca says.

Connecting with What Matters Most

Surviving cancer has given Rebecca a new perspective on just about every aspect of her life. "When you go through treatment for cancer, you think about doing as much as you can before your time runs out. Well that time is now!" She is intentional about making the most of every day, which may mean working with Mike to pack and ship boxes from their home office or taking an afternoon off to play with her children.

Though she's no longer in treatment, Rebecca finds it helpful to connect with other cancer survivors. "When you have cancer, you belong to a club that no one wants to be in. You feel a real connection with each other, like sisters, in the support groups." That connection continually affirms what she's doing with the care packages.

"All cancer patients have a moment when they need something to come in the mail to cheer them up," she says. And by sending them a little comfort, she knows she's making a big difference. "I am a very small piece of what is happening in those people's lives. I get immense pleasure from giving of myself to people who can really use and appreciate our packages. It has really helped me in my mourning process. I feel like I am sending a wink and a nod to Dad every time we send one out."

HAPPY ACT
Share Your Wisdom

What crisis have you survived or challenge have you overcome? The wisdom you've gained can help someone else. Volunteering with a charity or community organization can be a way to add meaning to your life by sharing your experience.

Dan Miller

Helping Others Succeed

Sometimes crisis is the impetus for discovering your purpose. Other times, your calling pursues you—even as you resist it. For Dan Miller, it was a little of both.

Dan was the son of a Mennonite preacher. Family and tradition forecast his future. He would help out on the family's farm after school and in the summer until he turned sixteen. Then he would be expected to quit school and work on the farm full-time.

That plan didn't work, however, for a young man with an entrepreneurial spirit (his first venture was selling Christmas cards door-to-door at the tender age of six) and an unquenchable curiosity about life. "There were never discussions about what are you gifted at or what your dreams were," says Dan. "To talk about considering leaving the farm was really heretical. Happiness wasn't part of the equation." Although doing so was discouraged, Dan kept exploring ways to see a little bit of the world beyond the family acreage. He fed his desire to see more, do more, have more, and be more by reading countless books.

And then, one day, he came across a recording of "The Strangest Secret," a motivational message by Earl Nightingale. Stealing away, the young teenager listened to the deep voice that told him again and again:

Success is the progressive realization of a worthy ideal. . . .
People with goals succeed because they know where they're
going. . . . We become what we think about. . . . Be of service . . . build . . . work . . . dream . . . create! . . . Your success
will always be measured by the quality and quantity of service
you render.[3]

The words took root in his heart and mind and affirmed that he wanted
to do something different—something that felt meaningful—with his
life. Concerned about his ideals, his parents sent him to a Mennonite
boarding school for his final two years of high school (the time during
which he should have been working full-time on the farm). "What they did
as a punishment ended up being an amazing experience for me. It opened
me up to encountering people whose theology wasn't that different from
my own, but they had a different view on life," Dan says. The experience
also confirmed his desire to break with tradition and go on to college.

From Crisis to Opportunity

Dan met his wife, Joanne, at college. During the next few decades, Dan
earned advanced degrees in psychology and counseling. He worked as a
therapist, a car salesman, and an entrepreneur starting multiple businesses
that met with varying degrees of success. From the outside looking in, his
life seemed to lack direction. But at home, the couple and their family
were happy as they explored each new opportunity, moved back and forth
across the country, and created a good life for themselves. Then, in 1988,
a financial crisis rocked their world. "I had leveraged one business into the
next and was in a vulnerable position when some banking regulations
changed. I ended up losing everything we had financially," Dan explains
in his book *48 Days to the Work You Love*.

During the ten years it took to climb out of a six-figure financial hole,
Dan, who had taken a job as a sales trainer, volunteered to teach a class at

his church about finding or creating work that is meaningful, enjoyable, and profitable. His message, which he based on personal experience, struck a chord, and attendees asked for the materials so they could share the information with family members and friends.

Serving by sharing what he'd learned through the years brought him joy. It gave his life a new, profound layer of meaning to know that what he taught helped people live fuller, richer, happier lives. So he put together a simple three-ring binder, recorded his talk on cassette tapes, and began selling them, not as a business but in response to people's needs. In fact, Dan felt reluctant about capitalizing on the course. "My whole [career coaching] path evolved without being a primary focus for me at all," he says. "Opportunities started exploding on the side that I thought of as community service. It took a while for me to get comfortable with that."

A New, Meaningful Direction

Ultimately, he did get comfortable with the idea, and in just three years he sold more than $2 million worth of those three-ring binders at an average price of $39 each—well over fifty thousand copies. With a heart for helping people get out of miserable jobs and find happiness in their work, Dan had finally found a very focused purpose. He has turned the initial course into a business that is both financially and personally rewarding.

"I've since encouraged a whole lot of people to look at where they are getting a sense of meaning, where they are serving best, and ask, 'How could I structure that skill or service so that I can create the income that I need?'" Coaching, writing, and speaking about how to find meaningful work became his full-time career. And it's one, he says, that keeps him on course in living a meaningful life. "Doing this is a reminder to me, day after day, to examine my life and think about my own passion and purpose." And day after day he is rewarded for his efforts. "Nothing fulfills me more than seeing the lights come on for somebody, for them to see the seed of an idea and put together a plan for it."

Some of the biggest lessons Dan has learned from his own life and from his experiences of helping others go back to the messages on that little record he found when he was thirteen. "Fulfillment comes from doing something that I would do even if money wasn't part of the equation," he says. "Happiness is a product of understanding your passion, doing something that has meaning, and serving others."

HAPPY ACT

What's Your Passion?

One way to identify what could bring (more) meaning to your life is to identify your passion. What do you enjoy doing? Who do you like spending time with? What would you do (or are you doing) for free because it's fun or important to you?

Of the activities you identify, which could you do more often in your work or spare time? Would doing so make your life feel more meaningful?

The Science Behind the
Wisdom of Meaning

It's a universal truth that meaning comes from serving or connecting to something other than yourself. A life focused solely on oneself can't leave a legacy; to make a difference, we must expand our own small lives by serving. That could mean helping with a cause, such as saving the planet or preventing animal cruelty. But most often your connection to other people will be the key to knowing your life makes a difference. As psychologist Michael Steger puts it, "Relationships are the ocean in which we find meaning."[4]

Steger's work affirms dependency between meaning and human connection. In one study he mentioned in his TEDx Talk at Colorado State University, he noted that almost 90 percent of people who were asked "What makes your life meaningful?" listed "other people" as their answer. Connecting with family and contributing to one's community and the world at large allows people to feel as if their lives matter. Your service might come through the contribution you bring to the world through your work, or it could be through involvement in your religious, social, or cultural community when you volunteer to teach children, visit the elderly, take food to those who can't get to the store, or work with teens as they explore what's next for their lives.

Psychologists and researchers have been studying meaning for more than fifty years and have found that it links to a variety of positive, happiness-boosting traits, including vitality, kindness, and resiliency. Several studies, such as one led by researcher Patrick Hill, of Carleton University in Canada, notes that meaning helps us live happier, *longer* lives. "Our findings point to the fact that finding a direction for life and setting overarching goals for what you want to achieve can help you actually live longer, regardless of when you find your purpose," says Hill. "So the earlier someone comes to a direction for life, the earlier these protective effects may be able to occur." The fourteen-year study of six thousand participants found a consistent correlation between the people's strong sense of purpose and longer life span.[5]

A study by Mount Sinai St. Luke's and Mount Sinai Roosevelt reports that a strong sense of purpose may also lower a person's risk of heart attack, and conversely a low sense of purpose may increase the risk of a cardiovascular event. Randy Cohen, a preventive cardiologist and coauthor of the study, says, "As part of our overall health, each of us needs to ask ourselves the critical question of 'Do I have a sense of purpose in my life?' If not, you need to work toward the important goal of obtaining one for your overall well-being."[6] Other studies show that living a meaningful life can help you live a healthier life, and may even lower your risk for Alzheimer's disease.[7]

How Do We Find Meaning?

Feeling as if your life has meaning clearly matters to your happiness and well-being. And it's interesting to note that this sense of meaning is a *feeling*—it is subjective. It isn't something you can purchase or be assigned or have given to you. It's something you have to discover for yourself. But how?

Do Something That Matters—to You

Although *meaning* and *purpose* aren't the same, they are quite often linked. Humans need to have purpose—a function to perform or service to provide—but your purpose and the meaning you derive from it can change depending upon your life stage or career.

For example, a stay-at-home mom of toddlers may have a very clear idea that her purpose is to raise and nurture tiny humans to grow into capable, thriving adults. As she watches her children grow and learn, she knows her care and attention are making a difference in their lives. A college professor with similar-age children may have the same goal for them, but see her purpose as being career-related. She finds meaning in the knowledge that her dedication helps young men and women prepare for their futures. A retired woman whose purpose is teaching English as a second language feels that her life matters, because she's helping her students open new doors of opportunity.

The women in these scenarios know their purpose and find significance as a result of doing work that matters—to themselves and others. Another person fulfilling one of these roles might feel bored and go through the motions of the work. Because meaning is subjective, you can find it doing something that others may think of as "just a job." The significance *you* ascribe to your work matters far more, with regard to finding meaning, than the work itself.

Studies from Gallup show that jobs are a prime source of meaning in our lives, so experts advise actively seeking meaning and purpose in your job, regardless of what it is. "Many people who don't have the job of their dreams can still find meaning by the way they approach it," says Sharon Salzberg, author of *Real Happiness at Work*. One way to change your outlook on work—and to increase happiness in the process—is to become more mindful and present. "Maybe it's by respecting and listening to customers. Maybe it's developing a sense of excellence at what you do, or choosing to treat people with compassion."[8] Changing how you approach the job can make a huge difference in how you feel about it—and determine how meaningful your work feels.

Look Beyond the Walls of Work

Work is one of the most common ways to live out your purpose and find meaning in life, but it certainly isn't the only one. For example, meaning can come from family traditions or may be rooted in spiritual or philosophical beliefs. Roy Baumeister, a professor of psychology at Florida State University, explains that meaning doesn't require a connection in the here and now. "Because it is not purely physical, it can leap across great distances to connect through space and time." Meaning's subjective, *felt* dimension allows us to connect the past, present, and future. He notes as an example that when modern Jews celebrate Passover or when Christians celebrate Communion, their actions are guided by symbolic connections to events in the distant past. "The link from the past to the present is not a physical one, the way a row of dominoes falls, but rather a mental connection that leaps across the centuries." Though those events are far removed by time, they provide a sense of meaning by anchoring millions of people's lives with belief in something much bigger than themselves.[9]

If you are seeking significance or want to create a life that feels worthy or important, looking beyond yourself to connect with and serve others is essential. If you have a good job—one that pays the bills and one where everyone gets along well—and still feel as if something is missing from your life, take a step back and evaluate your life and your connection to the world and people around you. What do you enjoy doing outside of work? Who are the people you feel the most energized by when you spend time with them? Do you have any hobbies or goals that involve or benefit other people?

"Sometimes people put undue pressure on their careers. Our work is only one tool for a meaningful life," Dan Miller says. "Look at other areas of life. What are you doing in other areas of your life to create meaning? Maybe you need to get involved in your church or community. What you perceive as a lack of significance may come from living your life too small."

get happy

Find your connection. Is your life connected to anything larger than yourself? Explore ways to get involved in your community, build your faith, or find a cause to actively support.

Seek to serve. Serving others is one simple way to make a difference in the world around you.

Find your purpose. You may not need a new job. A new perspective on your work can give you both a defined purpose and a sense of meaning. Why do you work? Who benefits from your efforts and how? What does the result of your work mean to others and to yourself?

Pass it on! What knowledge or talent can you share with others?

CREATIVITY

Creating is the act of paying attention to
our experiences and connecting the dots,
so we can learn more about ourselves and the
world around us.

—BRENÉ BROWN, *RISING STRONG*

*W*ho likes to draw?"

"Who is a good singer?"

"Who likes to write or tell stories?"

Ask any kindergarten class those questions and almost every little hand will shoot into the air. Ask a high-school class, and a few hands will go up, but tentatively—and likely accompanied by furtive glances to see if others' hands are raised. Pose those same questions at a business conference, and you'll be lucky to see one person raise a hand. And rather than looking to see if there are any other creative types in the room, that person will be watching to see if anyone is thinking "slacker" or doubting such a brash display of self-confidence.

In a culture that reveres productivity and busyness, creativity and play seem to be reserved for the young—or the foolish. Sure, a few lucky right-brained "creative types" can get away with painting for a living, but for the rest of us creativity is a luxury at best and, at worst, a waste of time.

Except, that's *not* true.

One of the definitions of creativity is "the ability to transcend traditional ideas, rules, patterns, relationships, or the like, and to create meaningful new ideas, forms, methods, interpretations, etc.; originality, progressiveness, or imagination."[1] That's something our world desperately needs! Thankfully, creative ability doesn't belong to the select few. *Everyone*—regardless of age, hair color, piercings (or lack thereof), style, or personality type—possesses the potential to be creative. That's why we see breakout novelists like John Grisham, Toni Morrison, Robert Ludlum, and Frank McCourt, who began writing seriously for the first time in their thirties, forties, or later. (We know a woman whose first book was published when she was ninety-three!) Grandma Moses started painting at age 75—and continued creating art until she passed away at age 101.

If the booming trend toward increasing numbers of DIY outlets and talent shows (think Pinterest, HGTV, and *America's Got Talent*) is any indication, people *want* to be creative. And rightly so! The *desire* and *ability* to create and innovate are part of our DNA. But busy schedules, conflicting messages about the value of creativity, and the tendency to compare our creations with others' (Hello, inferiority complex!), have a way of snuffing out this inborn gift. We want to give you permission to be okay with imperfection and to enjoy the creative process as you play, explore, experiment, and, yes, fail. Heck, post a picture online of your lopsided cake, misshapen pottery project, your rejection letter, or the warbly video in which you missed a few notes, and join millions of others who have learned to laugh at and grow from so-called failure. In truth, our creative mistakes often lead to new ideas and better techniques—so they can't really be called failures at all.

In this chapter, we'll introduce you to a few people who have tapped into their creativity at work and in their spare time to create a richer, fuller life experience. And although the examples shared here lean toward more traditional avenues of artistic expression, you'll also discover a few ways to awaken your creative spirit—even if you have no interest in picking up a paintbrush or writing the next great American novel. The amazing thing about this happiness-boosting practice is that the way you choose to express it can and *should* be as unique as you are.

Ben and Holly Raynes

Making Creativity a Priority

With careers in advertising, Ben and Holly Raynes needed to use their imaginations to succeed at work. But with demanding hours and two children under the age of four, there wasn't much space in their busy lives to replenish their creative energy, and even less time for play.

Holly edited and finished commercials for a postproduction company in Boston. She loved her work, but felt as though she was always rushing when it came to her daughters. "I rushed to pick up Amelie and Ivy from day care, rushed to feed them dinner, rushed to get them to bed. I was only seeing them when they were cranky, and they were only seeing me when I was cranky." But it wasn't simply the hectic schedule that made Holly grouchy. After work and kids, she felt as if there was "not an ounce" of her left for anything else. Writing had always been her hobby, but for three straight years she hadn't typed a word. "I was anxious, irritable, and antsy."

After too many rushed, crabby years, she and Ben knew something had to change. They sat down, looked at their budget, and determined they could survive on his salary. The necessary financial sacrifice felt like a fair trade for Holly's mental health. The next day, she sat across from the two owners of her company. "I haven't been doing so well lately," she began. Before she could resign, they stopped her. "We've noticed," they said. "We don't want to lose you, but we want you at your best." They offered her a part-time position on the spot. Instead of spending fifty-plus hours a week in the office, she'd be working twenty.

Prompting Creativity

It took a while before she felt revitalized enough to carve out time for writing. Despite working fewer hours in the office, her "free" time was spent taking care of chores at home that had been neglected for too long as well as caring for and playing with her daughters. The change of pace felt wonderful, but she found that the only days she could fit in writing sessions were Saturdays and Sundays when Ben could watch the girls. Two hours at a time, she sat in her favorite café, sipped a latte, lunched on curry, and forced herself to write, even if she didn't have anything to write about. "I used simple writing prompts such as 'What would happen if . . .' or 'She woke up and found . . .' just to get my fingers wandering over the keyboard until I would have a few hundred words."

Ben's Jewish grandmother had escaped Poland during World War II and had shared with Holly that, though she'd survived, she lost everything and everyone she had known. In her writing sessions, Holly began to wonder what it would look and feel like if something similar occurred in the United States. Soon she created a plot outline and developed character sketches. As she wrote, she'd slip into that state of flow where time ceased to exist as the images in her mind morphed into words on the page. "It felt so good to get my head into a creative space and have the time and energy to just go with it," she says. "I had been so discontent before, but I felt more and more invigorated after each writing session."

While she wrote, Ben took their daughters for bike rides or to get ice cream. Sometimes Holly felt bummed to miss out on the fun, and Ben says, "I was bummed she wasn't there too. But it was a sacrifice that was worth it for both of us. She was working on a gratifying project, and I could tell she was much happier and more fulfilled."

Once Holly was scratching her creativity itch, she noticed that Ben was getting antsy himself. "I could tell he needed something," she says.

"I felt fidgety, frustrated, and moody. I love my job, but I needed something else," Ben says. "Holly demanded I get a creative hobby." He began dabbling in watercolors. "I can't believe I'm saying this out loud, because I never remember my dreams, and I've never put any stock in them, but I started dreaming in watercolors. It sounds ridiculous, but I think I was tapping a creative part of my subconscious that had been dormant."

One night, he dreamed about a watercolor scene that moved. "The watercolor surfaces sort of came alive. I woke up at four in the morning and thought, 'How can I get my paintings to move?' I got out my little notepad and sketched out how it might work." He set up a workshop in an alcove of his and Holly's bedroom and started tinkering. He painted different parts of the same scene on multiple pieces of paper and then layered them together. Then, using gears he'd created with a 3-D printer, he made the scene come to life. His first moving painting depicted a boat sailing around an island.

Taking Turns for *Me Time*

Ben and Holly now take turns on the weekends, giving each other time for their creative pursuits. "It's not always easy to make the time, because there are so many priorities: your job, your kids, your marriage, your home, but *me time* is important too," Holly says. "If you don't take it for yourself, no one is going to give it to you. And when we come back together, we're happier."

They've also discovered that tapping into their creativity benefits their entire family. "Happy parents are better for kids," Ben says. "And it's been a great lesson to show our kids that it's important to do the things you love and to nurture your creativity." Following their example, Amelie (now eight) designs and sews her own clothes, and Ivy (now six) is an avid painter.

As for Holly's story idea inspired by Ben's grandmother? Her novel, *Nation of Enemies*, a political thriller, was published in 2015 under the name

H. A. Raynes. She's now at work on her second novel, sitting in her café, drinking lattes, and eating curry. Ben has made more than a dozen of his moving paintings and is building a large-scale version to be installed in the office of the Boston company where he works. Regardless of whether their projects had or will have any commercial success, they say that simply having a creative outlet makes an important difference in their lives. As Holly says, "Without it, we wouldn't be as happy and fulfilled as we could be."

HAPPY ACT
Schedule Some Fun!

Make an appointment with your creative,
playful self. Set aside time on the calendar this
week to do something you enjoy.

Stephanie Dolgoff

Writing Myself Happy

We'll let Stephanie tell her story.

"Just as a chef gets puffed up with pride when his restaurant gets a five-star review or a teacher feels accomplished when her struggling student has a lightbulb moment, as a writer, my work has always been something that has made me feel good about myself. Although not every article I write is a masterwork or even my own best work, during the twenty-five or so years I've been tapping away at my keyboard, I've learned I have a useful skill that I can rely upon to keep my kids in Converse and convey information to others in a way they tend to understand and appreciate. I'm proud of that and also relieved, because I'd be a horrible neuroscientist, electrologist, or really probably anything else (although I think I'd make a decent idle rich lady).

"But it wasn't until I wrote my book, *My Formerly Hot Life: Dispatches from the Other Side of Young,* five years ago that I realized that I'd also been confusing pleasure and happiness. Both are worthwhile pursuits. Although pleasure is certainly part of happiness, it isn't the whole enchilada. What I learned while writing the book—although sometimes not pleasurable—has had a lingering, life-changing effect that feels like I've turned a corner on the road to overall well-being that I hadn't known was there.

The Pleasure and Pain of Writing . . . and Waiting

"I'd written emotional, personal stories for magazines for years, in which I shared my inner self with my readers about my infertility, marital problems, an eating disorder from long ago. I always liked hearing that I'd helped others feel less alone in their problems. But those articles were always relatively short—three thousand words at most. The speedy feedback for what I wrote was like a quick high. First came the 'good job' from an editor, and then eventually a check.

"Later there were letters from readers. It's thrilling to hear that something you wrote made a stranger feel connected or less freakish and alone, and it's also nice to be validated in your point of view—especially if you're the one feeling like a freak. After the advent of social media, I relished the giddy hits of positive feedback I got when I posted a story. Cokeheads—and I swear I only know this from watching *Orange Is the New Black*—refer to a quick hit as a bump. Publishing and posting was my bump, and lots of little bumps definitely peppered my life with pleasure.

"Then I sat down and pumped out the several hundred pages of *My Formerly Hot Life,* which was released in 2010. Producing a book is obviously a much longer process in both the writing and the publishing—well over a year from idea to book signing. Sitting at the computer, day after day, digging in for what was a marathon, not a sprint, was challenging. I craved a bump. And though I did get a little encouragement from my editor as I wrote, sometimes weeks went by before she had read through my work. Sitting down and pushing through a longer narrative without the benefit of a 'nice work' or 'I loved that' from another pair of eyes meant that I had to find that encouragement and validation in myself. Sometimes it just wasn't there, perhaps because I'd come to rely on it from others.

"But I kept pounding away. Frustrating though it was at times, I started to enjoy myself. I forgot that I needed a bump or a thumbs-up—because I learned I was able to give it to myself. And as it turns out, it was a good thing that I broke my dependence on external validation.

"My book is a memoir about getting older—going from someone who was generally considered a 'hot' girl to a woman who gets asked the time from men who actually want to know the time, not to have sex! I wrote with what I thought was self-deprecating and relatable humor about the loss of something I had relied upon for most of my life. And I came to terms with the reality that no matter who we were when we were young, we all lose part of who we were with age, and we have to figure out who we are now.

"By and large, people loved the book. It was a *New York Times* bestseller, and I received wonderful mail and got to meet a few fans in real life. But there were a few people who reacted negatively, mostly to the idea that a woman felt highly enough about herself to acknowledge that she had been, in fact, 'hot.' Plus, how could I write about such vapid silliness when there was sex trafficking taking place in East Asia? And I called myself a feminist? Before the book was even available for review, there was a scathing piece in a popular online magazine accusing me of saying older women weren't hot (the opposite of the point of the book) and comments on another piece that featured my photo and said I needed a nose job, was a slut and an idiot, and had never been hot, not even when I was young.

Discovering a New Source of Meaning

"I can't say these digs didn't sting when I read them—sure they did, for a second or two. But surprisingly for someone who had come to realize she was addicted to the bump of praise, the disparagement felt like a mere annoyance. I also noticed that the positive feedback didn't give me the high it used to either. I was grateful, of course. I had showcased my soul for the world to see—in all its silliness, vanity, and general messed-up-ness—and the overwhelming response was 'thank you.' I loved being (mostly) appreciated for being me, but rather than a thrill, it felt more like a warm embracing confirmation of something I already knew.

"Positive psychology researchers have found that believing that your life has meaning is a big predictor of happiness, and the fact that I appeared to have been able to connect to others let me know I'd done something meaningful. But, for me, the most meaningful part of the creative process of writing a book was being able to connect with my own ability to say 'good job.'"

HAPPY ACT
Do Something That Makes You Stretch

You never know what you're capable of until you do something that takes you outside your comfort zone. To stretch your creative muscles, try a new challenge. Write in a different genre or format, try cooking a new recipe, work on solving a problem at work. Then, whatever your results are, pat yourself on the back for your efforts.

Billi Kid

Reinventing Himself

Stuck in "mediocre land," Guido Rodriguez dreamed of working on his own art in his home studio in Darien, Connecticut. Instead, the fifteen years he'd spent building a career as an art director in the marketing world had led to pitching fruit-flavored alcoholic beverages to sports-loving men. It wasn't the life he imagined when he planned a career as an artist.

As much as Guido loved the idea of creating his own art, he loved his wife, Claudia, and their two children more. As the family's sole bread-winner, he knew he couldn't give up his lucrative job—even if it was sucking the life out of him. He could have remained stuck and dissatisfied forever, had he not picked up a book that changed his life: *The Long Tail,* by Chris Anderson. In it, he read about a group of Boston-area musicians who cut a new door into the music industry. "It described how all these musicians created their own music by using an audio tool on their Macs. Then they used the Internet to reach their target audience," he remembers. Eschewing the traditional route, they skipped signing with a label and simply began creating and sharing their music with the world.

Inspiration dawned: he didn't need someone else's approval to pursue his art. Guido realized there was a way to express his unique creative personality without having to rely on art critics or gallery owners for exposure. Having grown up in Los Angeles and worked in New York City, he admired the bold graffiti artists who weren't trapped behind a desk all day. Filled with hope that he too could eventually escape the rat race, Guido tapped into his own interest in graffiti-style art and even created an alter ego for himself: Billi Kid.

Risking the Pursuit of Passion

After years of focusing on what others wanted him to create, Guido unleashed Billi Kid to explore his own style. But making the shift from a corporate employee to a full-time artist took a while. Guido held on to his full-time marketing job for four years while establishing himself as an artist. During that time, he used what he'd learned in marketing to connect with outlets to both display and sell his work. As his vibrant portraits and stickers earned press and started to sell, he found the courage to focus on Billi Kid's art full-time.

Leaving a "secure" job was risky. Darien isn't known for its low cost of living. And there was the daunting task ahead of him of putting his two kids through college. Naturally, his family had to be on board with his passion for Billi Kid; they would have to make sacrifices along with him. "My wife and kids have been very supportive. We've had challenges. Our idea of vacation has changed. I had to give up my strong health-insurance package," he says. But he and his family felt that pursuing a career that would allow him to create his own art was worth the risk. "We live in an affluent town, and we see all around us that money doesn't buy you happiness. Fulfillment of your goals is a huge part of happiness. Emotionally, this has been a great path for us."

"My first big break was having my work featured in *Time* magazine in an article about the grassroots interest in Barack Obama as a presidential candidate," he recalls. "Part of the article included some artists who were portraying him in unusual ways. My Billi Kid graffiti-style portrait of him was included. Next, I did a similar portrait of Michelle Obama for *New York* magazine." He's since both created and curated art for a number of organizations, including the NBA, Herman Miller, Gatorade, and Sprite. Billi Kid has exhibited work at Art Basel in Miami, Florida, and at

Barney's New York. And he recently finished a project with a powerful message about AIDS prevention. "The press from that project has connected me to philanthropic folks who have a charitable spirit and who can afford to buy my art."

Today, as Billi Kid, he continues to create his own art, and he curates the work of other urban artists. By combining his business experience with his passion, he discovered a way to make the kind of art he loves, earn a living doing it—and help others do the same. "I figured I could be Billi Kid the artist *and* be Guido the middleman, a creative consultant to companies that appeal to an urban lifestyle. I knew I could make a living doing it."

The art he curates can be found at Graffitication.com, an urban-inspired apparel site he launched in 2015. This new stage in his career took another leap of faith, since creating the site and buying the right high-tech printer required an investment—one for which he had to dip into his 401k savings. But he's optimistic about the new venture and hopes it will help him solidify his family's economic future.

"If not, it's all about reinventing yourself," Guido shrugs. "That's what's great about creative careers. Art keeps me young. That's what's so cool. I have all these kids who are fifteen years old who love my work. In what other career can you be an old fool and make young people happy? It's amazing. It keeps me going."

HAPPY ACT
Join a Club

Invite someone to get creative with you! Paint
with friends, join a book club, take a cooking class,
collaborate on a new project at work.

Levon Helm

Finding a New Voice

Nothing brought more joy to Levon Helm's life than music. He worked passionately his entire life to craft a career as a musician, overcoming streaks of bad luck and misfortune. So even when throat cancer stole his voice, he wasn't about to give up on his first love. Instead, he relied on music to sustain and heal him.

As a boy in Arkansas, Levon learned to play the guitar and mandolin and how to tear things up on the drums. He followed his creative muse from country fairs to the big city, where he ultimately found his home with the legendary rock group The Band.

Music was Levon's life, and The Band was his family. When its members went their separate ways, it crushed him. He knew he couldn't live without the joy music brought him, so he quickly recruited a new band, The RCO All-Stars. In short order, they played *Saturday Night Live,* cut an album, and booked a fifty-city tour. Shortly before the tour, Levon hosted a party in the dream home he'd built in Woodstock, New York. "It was one of those classic, golden, Catskill autumn afternoons," he later wrote. "The cider was cold, and the fried chicken was crispy. It felt like a dream had been realized." For a brief moment, everything felt right.

Unfortunately, despite the tour, The RCO All-Stars never took off. Music trends had changed. For a while, Levon succumbed to painful feelings of loss and failure and spent most of his time high and wasted. Music eventually put him back on the path to health and happiness: he realized that people still wanted to hear him sing and play, if in smaller numbers. Though that meant going back to the small venues, so be it; he was doing something he loved. Guitarist John Leventhal recalls playing in a pickup band behind Levon at a club in New Jersey: "It was a dive. A couple of the guys were complaining about what a dump the place was, but Levon just smiled and said, 'Come on, let's go make the people happy.'"

Rolling with the Punches

In January 1991, The Band reformed once again. New band members and a new record deal reinvigorated Levon's creativity. Misfortune, however, refused to yield and, in April that year, his beloved Woodstock home burned to the ground. Undaunted, Levon said, "Fire burned it. We'll build a better one."

His fortitude surprised friends and fans, but this attitude was typical of Levon. His stardom may have faded, but his creativity and passion remained strong. He played with The Band, contributed licks to the albums of friends, and sat in for a song or two at others' shows. In doing so, people developed a new appreciation for the unpretentious performer who cared more about the audience's enjoyment than himself. "He was the working musician's hero," says his daughter Amy. "He played wherever he could."

But another blow was waiting. In 1999, doctors diagnosed Levon with throat cancer. His doctor recommended removing his vocal chords, a choice that would have permanently ended his singing career. Instead, Levon gambled that twenty-seven radiation treatments would kill the tumors and preserve his voice. He was half right. The tumors disappeared, but doctors told him he would never sing again. Once again, he pulled himself up and drew on his creativity. Rededicating himself to drumming, he formed a new band fronted by his daughter Amy. Playing rejuvenated him. Despite all the loss, the cancer, heavy financial debt incurred from medical bills, and his inability to sing, he seemed more upbeat than ever.

Neither throat cancer nor the threat of foreclosure could stop Levon. To bring in money to cover his house payment, he got some musicians together and threw an old-fashioned rent party. Everyone had so much fun that he threw another. And another. Soon it became a regular thing. Levon dubbed the ongoing show the Midnight Ramble, and almost every week 150 people or so packed the rafters in Levon's home. Some of Levon's old pals made the trip from Manhattan to Woodstock to perform: first Emmylou Harris, then Dr. John, then Donald Fagen. Elvis Costello made an appearance, then Phil Lesh, Norah Jones, Mavis Staples, and many more. Midnight Ramble had morphed into a cool place to see legends up close and in the flesh.

Then something of a miracle happened. Little by little, Levon's singing voice returned. His once strong tenor had been replaced by something raspy and ornery, different but still compelling. Buoyed by this development, he took the act on the road, playing concert dates for large appreciative crowds. He made three more albums, each of which earned him a Grammy.

Levon kept playing until the spring of 2012, when relentless back pain revealed that cancer had returned, this time to his spine. At what would be his last concert, Levon, who seldom played encores, walked to the edge of the stage after the show and sang the Ralph Stanley spiritual "Gloryland." The song, which looks forward to a place where suffering is replaced by streets of gold, was something of a foreshadowing. A week later, Levon played his last ramble. Just before he passed away on April 19, 2012, he told family and friends: "Keep it going." Drawing on his music during the darkest times of his life, that is exactly what Levon managed to do.

HAPPY ACT
Plan a Jam Session

Learn a new skill or revisit an old hobby. If it's been years since you played the piano or strummed a guitar, sign up for a refresher course. Better yet, get the band back together.

The Science Behind the
Wisdom of Creativity

When Levon Helm faced foreclosure, he could have given up the home he loved. Instead, he looked at his options and at what he knew he could do. Using the resources he had—friends, music, and a place to play—he created a solution that saved his house and brought musicians and fans together in an intimate setting. When he turned the problem into an opportunity, two hundred people paid $100 each to pack into his home every Saturday night and helped bring him back from the brink of financial ruin. Levon's creative approach to life—one that he practiced and developed regularly through his music—helped his mind see new possibilities for solving his financial problems.

The ability to see life—or anything—from a new perspective is one of the many benefits of exercising your creative talents. Another is discovering a new sense of self-confidence from stretching and developing your abilities, as Stephanie Dolgoff did by writing a book. And for people who, like Guido Rodriguez and Ben and Holly Raynes, already *know* they have a creative bent but feel stifled by life and/or career choices, tapping into one's creative self, whether at work or in one's personal life, can be both liberating and stress relieving.

Writing, painting, and playing music are examples of artistic expressions of creativity, but they certainly aren't the only ways to express creativity. Cooking, running a business, or being a parent or grandparent can provide opportunities to shake things up; it isn't the activity itself that is creative—it's the way you go about it.

Creativity and Flow

Creativity is essentially the act of putting fresh, new ideas into action. Although scientists and artists may dispute the "true" definition of creativity, Shelley Carson, Harvard psychologist and author of *Your Creative Brain,* explains that creativity must have two specific components: it must be or involve something novel or original, and it must be useful in that it either benefits you or someone else.[2] That benefit could be something tangible, like crocheting a baby blanket to give to a new mom, or intangible, like the feeling of satisfaction that comes from pushing yourself out of your comfort zone. Or it could be the benefit of reinventing your career—or yourself. When creativity is viewed in that context, we can apply it to virtually any aspect of our lives.

Intertwined with the idea of creativity is the concept of *flow.* Researcher Mihaly Csikszentmihalyi notes in his book *Flow* that our best experiences come not when we are relaxed, but when we are exceptionally focused. "The best moments usually occur if a person's body or mind is stretched to its limits in a voluntary effort to accomplish something difficult and worthwhile."[3]

Flow is what happens when we become so completely engrossed in an activity that time seems to stand still or passes without our noticing. It's what Holly Raynes described when she talked about being immersed in her writing—when she gave herself over to the experience and, in her words, gave herself the "time and energy to just go with it." Once you get into flow, fingers fly over the keyboard, the imagination runs wild, and *voilà,* a novel is born. Or a masterpiece is created. Or a new app is launched.

In his book *The Rise of Superman,* Steven Kotler, journalist and director of research at the Flow Genome Project, explains that during flow the brain releases five neurochemicals: norepinephrine, dopamine, endorphins, anandamide, and serotonin. "All five affect performance," Kotler says.[4] Working in tandem, these hormones block out distraction, increase focus, improve pattern recognition, and enhance connection between ideas—even when those ideas seem unrelated at first.

"Once those creative juices start flowing, and you're no longer focusing on your own life or problems, you get into that flow state where you're working and the positive feelings are being reinforced," Shelley Carson says. "It's a great way to enhance your mood." Like a self-propagating cycle, our creative pursuits can lead to flow, which is followed by a happier mood, and when we are happy, we tend to be more creative.

Martin Seligman explains in *Flourish* that we don't necessarily have good (or bad) feelings while in this state, which scientists define as optimal consciousness. Following a period of flow, however, we often feel happier, less stressed, and generally more satisfied with life. Flow can lead to better creativity and productivity. It also has a happiness holdover effect that continues even after you return to less exciting or enjoyable tasks.

Why People Don't Think They're Creative

If the ability to create is indeed ingrained in our DNA, why do we so often hear (or claim), "I'm just not that creative"?

We Fear Failure or Rejection

Doing anything creatively involves risk, because it means stepping into unknown territory. What if your carefully planned meal doesn't end up looking picture-perfect? What if you launch a new initiative at work and it doesn't take off? What if you write an entire novel and your mom is the only one who reads it? What-ifs stifle creativity before it can even blossom. Instead of taking risks, we pick up a cake at the bakery, keep doing things the way they've always been done at work, and give up on the dream of being a bestselling author.

"By leaving the 'tried and true' pathway of action or thought, the individual exposes herself to possible failure and ridicule. That exposure is very anxiety-provoking for many people," Carson says. "People say 'I'm not creative,' but that's just not true. Every one of us is creative. The brain is a creativity machine. Some people may have been [criticized], so they decided they aren't creative, but that's truly not the case."

We Think Only Certain Types of People Are Creative

Researchers, including Rex Jung, assistant professor of neurosurgery at the University of New Mexico, and Randy Buckner, of the department of psychology at Harvard University, are studying what happens to the brain during the creative process—and finding that much of what we've believed is wrong. Their research is among the findings that displace the old notion of the right brain as our creative center and the left brain as analytical and logical. New studies show creativity engages the entire brain, with different regions working together during various stages of the creative process.[5] In other words, all of us have a creative network just waiting to be activated.

We're Busy Being Grown-ups

Misconceptions and stereotypes about what it means to be creative or an artist can also be inhibiting. Julia Cameron, author of *The Artist's Way*, explains that some people are hesitant to explore their creative side for fear it will ruin their stable life.

"We have a certain mythology around creativity that simply is not correct," she says. "We have been brought up to believe that artists are broke and tortured and crazy. When I say, 'Let's become an artist, let's play, let's get in touch with our inner resources,' people are frightened. They believe they can't be happy if they become an artist, but the opposite is true."

Julia believes that all of us are artists, regardless of whether we work at a kitchen stove, on a computer keyboard, on a blank canvas, or in a toolshed. "People who are developing creativity, allowing themselves to play and nurture creativity, are happier and more balanced," she says. "Artistic, creative people are solvent, they're happy; just start working on your creativity and watch what it does for you."[6]

Four Benefits of Creativity

Creativity improves your problem-solving skills. A study from the University of Toronto found that happy people are more creative, which in turn opens them up to new ideas or problem-solving capabilities.[7] Those ideas or solutions can then create more success and happiness, which further boosts their creativity. "It's a case of our own ingenuity and creativity driving more ingenuity and creativity," Shelley Carson says. "When you learn to use your creative brain more efficiently, there is no limit to the innovative ideas, products and new ways of doing things that you can explore."

Creating something with your hands, whether it's a painting or a meal, has proven psychological benefits that elevate your mood. In their book *The Creativity Cure,* Carrie and Alton Barron explain the correlation between happiness and using your hands: "Clinicians and research have discovered that weaving, sewing, and even chopping vegetables can be useful for decreasing stress, relieving anxiety, and modifying depression. . . . Creating something with your hands fosters pride and satisfaction, but it also allows you to physically express the things that spring up in your mind, in the moment."[8]

Ben Raynes discovered this truth for himself when he began creating his unique moving paintings. He didn't change his job or dramatically alter his life; he simply added a creative component to his life that stretched his thinking and problem-solving skills and allowed him to work with his hands. The difference he felt emotionally and mentally was significant enough that making time to create has become a priority in his life.

Learning a new skill or picking up a long-forgotten hobby stimulates new ways of thinking. If you take an art or cooking class, you may find yourself looking at things and asking, *What if? What if I tried this pattern instead of that one?* Or, *What if I added more or less of this ingredient?* Giving yourself the freedom to experiment—even if it's while you're doing something "just for fun," teaches your brain to look at life and its challenges from a variety of angles. In doing so, you gain a new perspective that may help you see beauty or opportunities that you may have otherwise missed.

Using your imagination allows you to discover new things about yourself. One of the keys to reconnecting with your creative nature is to give yourself some grace. Don't expect perfection—just play. Nashville-based artist Dorsey McHugh tells her painting students to view her classes as a time for exploration and discovery and above all to be ready to "rip up" their work. A study led by Paul Silvia at the University of North Carolina–Greensboro found that the *process of creating*—even when the attempts are "frivolous, amateurish, or weird"—is more important than the final product. "Engaging in creative pursuits allows people to explore their identities, form new relationships, cultivate competence, and reflect critically on the world," Silvia's team reports. "In turn, the new knowledge, self-insight, and relationships serve as sources of strength and resilience."[9]

How to Get Your Creative Juices Flowing

If you've been doing the same things the same way for years, you may not know *how* to break with routine. Just as creativity sparks innovation, the same ol', same ol' causes stagnation of thinking. Here are a few ways to shake things up and get your creative juices flowing.

Start Playing!

We are wired for playfulness. Even when we are babies, once our basic needs are met, our curiosity kicks in, and we start to explore. Play activates and produces circuits in our brain, especially in the prefrontal cortex, where judgment and planning occur. As children, we continue to learn by playing, by exploring and trying new things, as well as establishing an understanding of how to socialize and empathize with others.

"Play is built into [our] biology in a very deep way," says Dr. Stuart Brown, founder of the National Institute for Play and author of *Play*. "As we look at the biology of nutrition and the biology of sleep, the things that we humans need to survive, play is not normally considered something important. But when you look at a life without play, particularly when a child is developing, you can begin to see the consequences of play deprivation, which also begins to show you the benefits of play."[10]

Through four decades of research into the play histories of convicted murderers, Stuart found that the suppression of childhood play led to violent and antisocial behavior. Conversely, he found that fulfilled and successful people were more engaged and optimistic if their history included a healthy amount of play. Playful people tend to be more flexible and adaptable to evolving situations.

Although play is more prevalent during childhood for learning and skill development, it continues to benefit our well-being throughout our lives. But when you think of play, activities such as running through the sprinklers, pretending to be Wonder Woman or the Hulk, or playing Chutes and Ladders may come to mind. Childhood games were fun— when we were children. Now, playing Chutes and Ladders with your kids or grandkids can feel mind-numbingly boring (although precious smiles on tiny faces help make up for the monotony) and singing into a hairbrush just seems silly.

But playing doesn't have to be child's play. Anything you do for the sake of doing and that gets you into a state of flow is considered play. Reading a book for pleasure, crocheting a blanket, hiking through the woods, dancing with someone you love, enjoying a game of tennis or round of golf with a friend (and not keeping score) are all ways to play. The point is to do something that gives you joy simply because you enjoy doing it.

In Holly Raynes's case, writing equaled play. Although we hope her books are a huge success, she didn't start out with dreams of becoming a bestselling author. She simply recognized a hole existed in her life of all work and no play. She's not alone. Fifty-two percent of Americans say "lack of time" is their biggest barrier to practicing creativity.[11] To get back to writing, a hobby she thoroughly enjoyed but set aside while she built a career and tended to her family, she had to intentionally carve time out of her schedule to write. But even with that dedicated time, it took effort to coax the words from her brain. If the busyness of life has kept you from practicing a hobby, don't be surprised if you feel a bit rusty when you begin again. Holly Raynes used writing prompts to get her fingers "wandering over the keyboard." And she ultimately discovered the act of writing *for her own enjoyment* stirred her creative juices and brought joy into her life.

Ben Raynes experienced a similar creativity-happiness connection when he began working out what it would take to create moving paintings. The satisfaction that comes from creating—whether it's words on a page or a painting—carries over into other areas of their lives.

"Play precedes happiness, and it is a building block to happiness," Stuart says. "Really having a sense of fulfillment and joyfulness requires that we honor and stay close to our own personal proclivities and our personal play nature. I think play and happiness are partners."[12]

Do a Little Daydreaming

Creativity, like happiness, isn't necessarily a task that can be tackled head-on. Sometimes a more fruitful approach is to let your mind wander and slowly explore an idea. Scott Barry Kaufman, an NYU psychology professor, and psychologist Rebecca McMillan coauthored a paper titled "Ode to Positive Constructive Daydreaming," noting that some people spend as much as 50 percent of their waking hours daydreaming.[13] Although that may sound excessive, take a look at a few of the potential rewards they say can come from daydreaming:

Self-awareness

Creative incubation

Improvisation and evaluation

Goal-driven thought

Unfocused thinking time, like the moments you spend taking a shower, walking your dog, or working in your garden, may provide the perfect opportunity for your brain to come up with an innovative solution or idea for a new project.

Turn on the Tunes

"Music is one of the most exquisitely effective ways of allowing you to enter the mind-wandering mode," says Daniel Levitin, author of *This Is Your Brain on Music*. "You relax and you let your thoughts flow from one to another, and that's how you get into creativity."[14]

get happy

Daydream. Find a quiet space and let your mind wander, question, and invent without boundaries.

Be curious. It's easy to think, "Been there, done that" in your daily routine. Rather than walking mindlessly through your day, take notice of the way things work (or don't work) in your home or office. Ask, "Why do we do it this way?" "Why do I take this route to work?" "Is there another way to do this?"

Learn something new. Take a class or find a YouTube video to help you master a new skill.

Make a creativity playlist of your favorite instrumental music and allow your mind to wander . . . and create.

Give yourself time to get into flow. Getting into flow, that optimal state of consciousness, isn't like flipping a light switch. It requires a bit of time and concentration. To get in the zone, find a quiet place to work or put on music that helps you block out distractions, so you can really focus on your creative task.

Have fun! Play a game, swing with your kids at the park, schedule time for a hobby you enjoy.

GRATITUDE

Gratitude makes sense of our past, brings peace for today, and creates a vision for tomorrow.

—MEGAN BEATTIE

*T*hank you."

Whether whispered with a kiss, exclaimed with joy, or delivered with a handshake, these two little words hold incredible power. In an instant, they acknowledge and encourage the recipient; *everyone* likes to feel appreciated. But the act of saying thank you has its most significant effect on the speaker. More important than the words themselves is the gratitude that fills them with meaning. Spoken aloud, written on the page, or acknowledged silently as in prayer, genuine gratitude can enhance the way you see the world, increase and renew your hope, and fill the empty places in your heart.

"Gratitude is many things to many people," writes Sonja Lyubomirsky in *The How of Happiness*. "It is wondering; it is appreciation; it is looking at the bright side of a setback; it is fathoming abundance; it is thanking someone in your life; it is thanking God; it is 'counting blessings.' It is savoring; it is not taking things for granted; it is coping; it is present-oriented."[1] Some people call it an attitude, some call it an action, and some call it an emotion. Regardless of the terms used to describe it, gratitude is a person's choice to look for the good in life.

Gratitude is, perhaps, one of the easiest happiness practices to add to your life, because there is *always* something for which to be grateful. (Don't believe us? Joan Lewis, one of the people whose stories you'll read in this chapter, sparked a global gratitude movement after receiving word that she had just two weeks to live.) It's also an easy habit to adopt, because it offers an immediate physical and emotional reward. Think about it. It's difficult, if not impossible, to feel discouraged and grateful at the same time. When you notice the good in the world, you immediately feel better.

For those for whom gratitude is a way of life, the benefits are even greater. Studies have revealed that grateful people experience improved immunity, better sleep, and lower blood pressure. They are also better equipped to overcome mild to moderate depression and improve their relationships.

Although saying thank you is a good start, becoming a grateful person—one whom Robert Emmons describes as a person who receives and accepts all of life as a gift—doesn't happen overnight. It does, indeed, require practice. Emmons, who is the editor in chief of the *Journal of Positive Psychology* and a psychology professor at the University of California–Davis, explains that the practice of gratitude comprises two key components: affirming the goodness in the world around you and recognizing that the source of this goodness is something outside yourself.[2]

In the pages that follow, you'll read about people who have chosen gratitude as a way of life. They, perhaps like you, have experienced hardship, loss, and grief and endured common and extreme challenges. Those experiences, paired with the intentional choice to look for the good in every situation, have led them to discover that gratitude may well be the simplest path to happiness. As you begin your own journey toward life-long happiness, we hope you'll choose this path as well.

Ryan Bell

Giving with a Thankful Heart

Choosing to be happy and thankful is deliberate for Ryan Bell, a teen who, despite his insistence to the contrary, is anything but ordinary. Ryan was born with the craniofacial disorder Treacher Collins syndrome (TCS), a condition that affects the bone and soft-tissue formation of the face. His eyes slant slightly downward, and his cheeks, jaw, and ear bones are malformed. His underdeveloped jaw affects his airway, speech, and eating and, until Ryan was twelve, required him to have a tracheotomy to breathe. The malformation of his ears caused significant hearing loss and requires him to wear special hearing aids.

But to suggest it is Ryan's appearance that makes him unique would be misleading. His struggles—from the forty complicated and painful surgeries he's endured to learning to navigate a curious and at times unkind world—have instilled in him a unique perspective on suffering and gratitude.

Ryan learned at an early age that he could choose how to view his circumstances. "I understand now how lucky I have been. If I had been born into a family living in an [impoverished] area that [the charity] Heifer helps, I'm sure that I wouldn't have survived because of my medical issues. I live twenty minutes from Yale New Haven Hospital. I stopped breathing at home, and my father had EMT experience and saved my life. I needed machines and tubes and medicines and medical equipment and nursing and therapy—that kind of help isn't available everywhere."

Ryan and his parents could have hidden away in their own little world and asked, "Why us? Why Ryan? Why so much pain?" But they chose a different approach to life—one that acknowledges the blessings in their own lives and, in response, focuses on what they can do to help others.

To live out this mind-set, the Bells started a family tradition several years ago of giving back at the holidays. In 2009, when a Heifer International gift catalog arrived in the mail, Ryan, who loves animals, immediately began lobbying for Heifer to become the family's charity of choice that year. The nonprofit's mission is to end hunger and poverty by providing gifts of livestock along with training on how to care for the animals. The sheep, goats, llamas, cows, geese, chickens, water buffalo, and camels can be bred and the offspring or meat sold. Some of the animals provided by Heifer International are used to plow fields and supply fertilizer for crops, while others are sustainable sources of wool, eggs, and dairy products that families can use themselves or sell for income.

The following year, 2010, Ryan wanted to support Heifer International again. This time he set out to raise money for the organization by helping run a family friend's booth at a craft fair. She sold her creations, and he talked about his fund-raiser for Heifer—a daunting task for any ten-year-old, but one especially difficult for a child with impaired speech. The experience pushed him out of his comfort zone, something that he is grateful for now, even if he was initially hesitant. "I get nervous speaking to new people, because I'm not sure they will understand me. This project made me really work on this. It was hard, but watching the results of the fund-raising was worth it. I knew I was helping other people. I didn't know who these people were or what they were going through, but helping others made me happy," he says.

Inspired to Help a Village

In 2011, he determined to go even bigger. Ryan's goal was to buy a camel—or to donate $850. Ryan's mom, Laura, says the project was an incredible boost that provided him with "his own little 'project world,'" where he felt accepted and appreciated by others. Teaming up with his younger sister, Meghan, Ryan collected donations from friends, family, and even strangers who heard about the boy who initially wanted to donate $850 to buy a camel for a family in need. They raised nearly $9,000 for the organization that year.

Their fund-raising success drove them to push for more in 2012. It was a difficult year medically for Ryan. Jaw surgery caused him to miss five weeks of school, and he had to relearn how to eat and talk. When he returned to school, his teachers and classmates fussed over his new appearance—his jaw had been forced forward, a procedure that allowed him to breathe without the tracheotomy. His own physical transformation inspired him to increase his goal and help even more people through Heifer International's "Gift of Transformation." The fund-raising level carries a price tag of $25,000, but when Ryan saw the name of the gift, it resonated with him.

"I was excited when I saw the Gift of Transformation in the gift catalog, because it reminds me of the transformation that I went through. I want to give my own Gift of Transformation to the world. I want to send herds of heifers, llamas, and goats, flocks of sheep and chickens, a pen of pigs, a school of fish, and a gaggle of geese to an underdeveloped area of the world and let a transformation take place as the gift is received, utilized, and passed along. A Gift of Transformation can affect the lives of people in an entire village or community."

To date, Ryan and Meghan have doubled the goal and are now hoping to send two Gifts of Transformation to the developing world. The funds are tracked on their "team" page at Heifer.org/RyanBell (donations can be made there as well). Still a few thousand dollars short of the overall $50,000 goal, Ryan says it doesn't matter how long it takes to reach that mark. "I don't want people to suffer even if I have to," he says. "I'm happy with who I am."

HAPPY ACT
Give Thanks

Like Ryan, you can focus on your struggles or you
can count yourself lucky for everyday blessings.
If you're dealing with a challenge, it can be helpful
to shift your focus to something positive.
Right now, stop and think of one good thing in
your life for which you're thankful.

Kristin A. Meekhof

The Healing Power of Gratitude

Kristin tells us her story.

"Grief, I believe, has a texture of roughness. Like a blanket of sandpaper, it envelops one's entire body. People don't know how to approach a person prickled with pain, so they keep their distance. After all, who really wants to hug a porcupine?

"I was that porcupine in 2007 after my husband, Roy, passed away approximately eight weeks after being diagnosed with adrenal cancer. I was thirty-three at the time.

"The sharp quills, well, that's what grief creates. The emotions and the spikes they form don't always appear immediately. In my case, it was a few weeks after the funeral that the feelings of anger, disappointment, shock, despair, and depression slowly started to emerge and isolate me physically and mentally.

"When you are the porcupine, you are fully aware that no one knows how to handle you. All you want is to be hugged. You want someone to wrap their arms around you, but people are afraid to even sit beside you.

"In my own life, gratitude was the one thing that relieved the pain of grief. Making lists of who and what I was thankful for gave me a perspective of hope—of healing. I can still remember the first gratitude list I wrote through teary eyes after Roy died. Let me tell you, it wasn't easy.

But I asked myself, 'What would Roy want me to do?' And I *knew* he would say, 'Make a gratitude list.'

"It was Roy who introduced me to the concept of practicing gratitude. We were talking over coffee a few months before we were married, and I was having a pity party for myself. He interrupted me mid-sentence, something very unusual for him to do, and told me, in no uncertain terms, that I had too much to be grateful for to be upset by 'life's minor inconveniences.' I bit my tongue so hard I thought I would need surgery. But I realized he was right. From that point on, we regularly exchanged gratitude lists via e-mail.

Finding Comfort, List by List

"Years later, Roy and I had a similar conversation. Again, it was over coffee, but this time he was sitting in a wheelchair and we were at the University of Michigan's cancer center. I noticed he wasn't drinking his coffee and asked if he wanted something different. His answer wasn't what I expected. He told me he wanted me to start making a gratitude list. I'm sure the glare I gave him in response did some damage. I already felt stretched to my outermost limits dealing with the news of his terminal cancer and working as his primary caregiver. Now he wanted me to add gratitude to my to-do list? I was ready to push the nuclear button.

"Roy held firm; he started the gratitude list right then and there in the hospital. 'They [the medical staff] got us in before everyone else this morning. You've really learned how to navigate your way around this place.' He grabbed my hand and added, 'We have each other.' In that moment, my husband taught me that gratitude is the answer to every question.

"Grief left me ragged; gratitude helped to smooth the rough edges. In the weeks and months following the funeral, I made list after list of everything for which I could still be grateful. Those small and good things softened me and helped me see new opportunities for life. Gratitude allowed grace to permeate the quills and, slowly, they began to disappear.

"I can't explain how gratitude works; it seems to have an almost mystical quality. But I do know that when you practice being thankful, especially during the harshest of circumstances, the act of recognizing the good in life allows healing to begin. In many ways, gratitude gave me new life.

"About three and a half years ago, I decided to interview widows about what grief has taught them. I wanted to compile their nuggets of wisdom into a book that would help others in their own journey of healing. I discovered that, although there are many elements to resilience and well-being, the widows who actively practiced gratitude found joy once again. Sure, they still experience rough patches, but these women know the same healing truth that Roy revealed to me that day in the cancer center: gratitude is the answer to every question."

HAPPY ACT
Count Your Blessings

Make a list—right now—of at least five things
or people for whom you are grateful.

Brandon Mancine

Committed to Gratitude

The happy, successful life Brandon Mancine enjoys today as a fitness and nutrition professional in San Antonio, Texas, is a far cry from that of his childhood. Raised by his grandparents in a poor area of southwestern Pennsylvania, he constantly felt disappointed with the hand life had dealt him. In hopes of escaping what he saw as a dead-end life, Brandon joined the Marines after high school. It was a decision that put him on a path to a completely new outlook on life—it also kept him alive and out of trouble.

"The year after high school four of my friends died and several went to jail," Brandon recalls. "I have no doubt I would have been one of them, if I hadn't entered boot camp just days after graduation."

Brandon had grown up listening to military stories about his grandfather's Marine Corps service as a machine gunner in World War II. Brandon enlisted for four years, determined to become a machine gunner like his grandfather. Boot camp challenged him physically and mentally in preparation for battle, but it didn't prepare him for the reality check he would get during his tours of duty.

Brandon's first six-month deployment after boot camp was to the Middle East, where he saw examples of poverty far worse than he could have imagined in Pennsylvania. Remembering the first time he got "liberty"—time off to leave the Marine base and explore the area—he says, "We were in the Persian Gulf country of Bahrain, which at the time in the late 1990s was known for widespread human-rights violations. There was absolutely no middle class. Everyone was either very poor or very rich. As we wandered through the markets, we saw many desperate beggars amid the wealthy shoppers. There was this one woman lying by the side of the road with her disabled son. I was horrified to see everyone was just stepping over her. But whenever anyone would give her anything, she showed such pure joy and thanks. It was such a little amount, but it made her so happy, and I thought, 'What do I have to complain about?'"

Another jarring memory for Brandon was during a deployment to Japan. "We were headed to Mount Fuji for survival training. When we landed, we took the bus to the base. Along the way, we saw some pretty dilapidated living conditions that seemed even worse than what we were training for. And yet these families were living in them. That was a real gut check," he recalls.

Determined to Be Grateful— for the Good *and* the Bad

Throughout his four years in the Marines, Brandon saw and met people who continued to make him feel more grateful about what he had. "I encountered so many people worse off than I was, yet they found ways to be happy," he says. But poverty wasn't his only teacher. The lessons also came from examples of *un*gratefulness. "There was one guy in our unit who was always complaining. We used to say he had a problem for every solution." Brandon realized he'd been guilty of that same ungrateful attitude toward his childhood.

Somewhere between the destitute and discontented, Brandon realized that entitlement—the feeling that he deserved more or better—had made him unhappy for too long. Seeing others who endured dire circumstances, he finally understood how much he had to be grateful for. After years of complaining about what he didn't have, he decided to shift his focus to gratitude. "You have the option to put what you want into your life, to make the best out of things," he says. With that decision, he determined to be thankful for everything—good or bad—that came his way. "Happiness isn't just bouncing around and smiling all the time. It's appreciating even the things in life that may not seem so idyllic."

For the past ten years, Brandon has *practiced* gratitude, meaning he's developed habits that help him constantly be aware of the good things in his life. He uses meditation each morning as a way to both clear his mind and maintain a perspective of thankfulness. And every evening he and his wife, Tara, take a gratitude walk. "When the day is winding down, it's really easy to think about what went wrong," Brandon says. He remains true to his commitment to gratitude by choosing to focus on what went right. "We go out for a fifteen-minute walk and take turns listing out loud the good things that happened that day and the things in life we're grateful for—our home, our health, our family."

How can others get to this grateful place? "Just start," Brandon tells everyone. "Start looking for something to be thankful for, start looking for someone to compliment. The more you do it, the more you'll see what you have in life."

HAPPY ACT
Take a Gratitude Walk

Go for a walk with your spouse, child, parent, or
friend. Take turns noting things you're grateful for.

Joan Lewis

The Power of Gratitude

When the doctors told Joan Lewis on September 17, 2009, that end-stage pancreatic cancer had spread to her liver, they warned her she only had a couple weeks to live. Joan, a grandmother from Pringle, Pennsylvania, didn't want her loved ones to dwell on the bad news. She told them, "Don't make a fuss. Just do something nice for somebody else. Then tell me about it."

Her daughter Jacqueline shared Joan's wish with a few people, and they in turn told others. Before long, people in all fifty states had responded by doing a good deed in honor of "Joannie from Pringle." Eventually, people from all seven continents, including Antarctica, sent Joan notes. Daily, missives about small acts of kindness cheered the retired teacher, who read them over and over.

"An acquaintance of mine didn't have enough to eat the past few weeks, so I stopped off with a few bags of groceries, Joan," wrote Julia Kristan on Joan's page at CaringBridge.org.

"I took notice of one of the poor crossing guards who looked very cold and wet . . . so I stopped and got her a coffee," shared a Connecticut resident on the Joannie from Pringle Facebook page. "She was very grateful!!!"

"Sent a letter to a soldier I didn't know," wrote another.

"When I went grocery shopping, I picked up an extra bag of food and cleaning products for an out-of-work friend," wrote someone in Pennsylvania.

Days passed, and Joan was overwhelmed by the response to her request. "I cannot believe what an outpouring of love and laughter has come my way," Joan wrote on CaringBridge one month after receiving the diagnosis. "I especially love the notes from people who tell me what they have done for Joannie from Pringle," she noted. "Such creative deeds, and I feel blessed to know they are done in my name."

By that time, Joan had defied the two-week prognosis and felt well enough to cross a few items off her bucket list. She floated in a hot-air balloon in Charlottesville, Virginia, where she was staying with her daughter Jocelyn. The next week, she joined friends on a trip to New York City and watched ABC's *The View* from a second-row seat—close enough to see Barbara Walters's red strappy shoes in detail.

Starting a Gratitude Movement

Months passed, and her positive outlook, bolstered by news of good deeds and gratitude, helped Joan tolerate chemotherapy and continue to beat the odds. The effect that the hope-filled stories had on her mother inspired her daughter Jacqueline to create a World Gratitude Map (https:// gratitude.crowdmap.com/). The crowd-sourced website invites users to briefly share a good deed or word of thanks and stick a virtual pin to mark their location. Jacqueline reasoned, if her mother has survived so long by focusing on good deeds, why not start this map so everyone could focus on the positive and feel good? Knowing that public-health practitioners use maps to track bad things such as flu outbreaks, Jacqueline decided to track good things instead. Adopting the motto "Gratitude is contagious," she launched the site in October 2010, more than a year after her mother was told she had two weeks to live. And once again, positive notes poured in.

"Grateful for job after six months of unemployment!!!" wrote someone in St. Simons, Georgia.

"I am grateful that my mommy helped me with my math homework," wrote a Floridian.

"Happiness is a totally unexpected two-hour late-night chat with a college bestie," wrote someone in North Decatur, Georgia.

"Happy birthday to my Dad, the very best man I have ever known and the most loving father anyone could ever have. I am so grateful for you," wrote a New Yorker.

"I'm thankful my boss/landlord helped me get an apartment, so my boys and I wouldn't be homeless. I still need a warm place for my chickens," jotted another.

These people, along with more than forty-two hundred others, offered proof that gratitude can be not only contagious, but life-changing as well. "The stories we tell create the people we become," Jacqueline explains.

All that gratitude certainly changed the way Joan lived her final days. "These last eighteen months have been like Tom Sawyer's funeral, a chance to hear and be surprised by people thanking me for affecting them," she told a reporter from the *Citizen's Voice* in Wilkes-Barre, Pennsylvania. "I am so blessed, the luckiest woman on earth, really."

Joan's body eventually succumbed to the cancer. At age seventy-four, she passed away on May 7, 2011. "She didn't die in two weeks. She lived for twenty months, outperforming the prognosis by any stretch of the imagination," said Jacqueline in an interview with a South African radio station: "I believe it was because these good things kept her going—this ability to see the good in the world."

HAPPY ACT

Post a Note of Happiness or Gratitude

Visit HappyActs.org and take the #HappyActs challenge. Post a note on Twitter, Facebook, or Instagram about something you've done to make someone smile or share what someone has done to make you smile. Be sure to tag your post with #HappyActs.

The Science Behind the
Wisdom of Gratitude

The study of gratitude, its importance, and its benefits began in earnest within the scientific community in 2000. Prior to that, although philosophers and religious leaders had taught for centuries about the importance of giving thanks, neither group could provide concrete data on why or how gratitude contributes to well-being. That changed in October 2000, when The Templeton Foundation brought together a small group of scientists in Dallas, Texas, for the purpose of advancing the science of gratitude. The reason for their interest is summed up in part with this quote from the late philanthropist Sir John Templeton: "When we fill our minds with blessings and gratitude, an inner shift in consciousness can occur. As we focus on the abundance of our lives rather than what we lack, a wonderful blueprint for the future begins to emerge." Templeton understood what scientists can now explain with empirical data. Gratitude has the power to improve people's lives by changing their perspectives and, thereby, their attitude and actions.

How Gratitude Affects the Body and Brain

It's easy to recognize the correlation between happiness and a grateful attitude. You *feel* those happy vibes each time you make even a small gesture of thanks. But understanding, from a scientific standpoint, why and how gratitude affects people over weeks, months, or a lifetime has taken much research. And because of this happiness practice's profound impact on well-being, the research is ongoing. By studying chemical reactions in the brain and the rest of the body and by conducting numerous social and psychological experiments, neurologists and psychologists have learned that gratitude causes both a physical and an emotional response.

Scientists have learned, for example, that people with higher gratitude levels show more activity in the hypothalamus. That's important, since the hypothalamus is the control center for everything from functions like eating, drinking, and sleeping to metabolism and stress levels. Stimulating the hypothalamus with gratitude has proved to improve sleep, lessen physical discomfort, and lower stress and anxiety.

Gratitude is also acknowledged by scientists for its immune-boosting effects. A study by Robert Emmons and Michael McCullough found that people who counted their blessings on a regular (daily or weekly) basis reported fewer aches and pains and better sleep than people who focused more on life's burdens.[3]

Again, gratitude is a habit that's easy to develop. The reason? Your body rewards your words of thanks with a happiness-boosting shot of dopamine. Put simply, demonstrating gratitude feels great. And since it feels good, we are prone to practice it again and again.[4]

It's great that being grateful can increase immunity. But can a person who suffers from chronic or even terminal illness benefit from practicing gratitude? Without question.

For example, in one study, Fuschia Sirois, a professor in the department of psychology at Bishop's University in Sherbrooke, Quebec, and Alex Wood, director of the Behavioral Science Centre at the Stirling Management School at the University of Stirling in Scotland, conducted research on the role of gratitude in people with chronic illness. Sirois and Wood compared patients who practiced gratitude with those who practiced benefit finding, which involves looking at what they have gained from their experience. The researchers found the gratitude group enjoyed significantly greater well-being and were less vulnerable to depression.[5]

"One of the most striking findings was the consistent benefits of gratitude for reducing depression over time," Sirois says. "This is very important for individuals living with chronic illness, as depression rates tend to be much higher compared to those without ongoing health issues. Learning to notice all the small but positive things in one's life is key for enhancing happiness and well-being. When this becomes habitual, it can improve mood and adjustment."

The findings, which Sirois calls "very promising," align with Joan Lewis's experience. Rather than focusing on her terminal diagnosis of pancreatic cancer, Joan turned her attention toward more positive things. Writing notes of thanks on her CaringBridge page and reading the messages from others about their good deeds and moments of gratitude lifted her spirits. Her daughter Jacqueline told a reporter who interviewed Joan at a University of Connecticut NCAA women's basketball championship game, "Only my momma can make dying look like a party you wish that you were invited to."

Death, a party? It all depends on how you look at life. Over and over again, Joan read the notes that people posted about the good deeds they'd done and the gratitude they felt or received. Those notes made her feel both grateful and happy. Her body responded to the medicinal and emotional care in a way that surprised her and her doctors—giving her twenty months, instead of two weeks, to live. Can that extra time be directly attributed to gratitude? Perhaps not, but there is little doubt that it contributed to a happier state of mind during a time when many people would have felt distraught or suffered from clinical depression.

Good for the Soul

Not unlike Joan, Kristin Meekhof experienced the power of gratitude when applied as an emotional balm. Both women experienced difficult circumstances and found gratitude to be a source of strength and healing. In neither case did recognizing the good in their lives make the bad go away. Gratitude doesn't work that way; it isn't a magic pill. However, practicing gratitude does helps us all overcome what psychologists call our negativity bias—a natural tendency to remember negative experiences over positive ones. And as Kristin discovered by focusing on what she was grateful for, maintaining a *positive* bias can help you move forward after failure, loss, or hardship.

Multiple studies affirm that developing an abiding sense of gratitude strengthens one's ability to bounce back after even the hardest hits. A 2003 study in the *Journal of Personality and Social Psychology* found gratitude was a major contributor to resilience following the terrorist attacks on September 11. Another study, published in *Behavior Research and Therapy* in 2006, found that Vietnam War veterans with higher levels of gratitude were less likely to experience posttraumatic stress disorder.[6]

Good for Your Relationships

Science makes it clear that gratitude is good for both physical and emotional health. Likewise, demonstrating thanks to the people in your life—whether they are family members, friends, or coworkers—has a measurable, positive effect on those relationships. The simple explanation for this is that a person who acknowledges and appreciates others is more likable. People enjoy being around people who are positive and kind. In contrast, we tend to avoid those who continually complain.

In relationships, both the way we respond to one another and *why* we respond the way we do can either strengthen or damage our bonds. For example, thanks given out of a sense of indebtedness, obligation, or quid pro quo can have a negative effect on the relationship—particularly in close or romantic relationships.

In a study titled "It's the Little Things: Everyday Gratitude as a Booster Shot for Romantic Relationships," researchers asked couples to track their feelings of gratitude and indebtedness daily. A sense of obligation to return a favor led to neutral or negative feelings toward the relationship, but a feeling of gratitude *enhanced* the way partners felt about each other and the relationship in general. Researchers noted: "Women's increased feelings of satisfaction with the relationship and men's increased feelings of connection to the partner and satisfaction with the relationship were predicted by gratitude felt on the previous day." And the acts for which each felt grateful were "little things" like picking up their spouse's favorite drink from Starbucks or giving the other a break of an hour or two from the children. The researchers concluded: "Gratitude may help to turn 'ordinary' moments into opportunities for relationship growth, even in the context of already close, communal relations."[7]

That study and others reveal that gratitude is necessary for healthy relationships. Here's the bad news—or the opportunity for improvement—people, in general, don't say thank you enough to the people closest to them. In one survey, 90 percent of respondents said they were grateful for their families, but only 76 percent shared their gratitude with their children and even fewer, 49 percent, told their parents. At work, only 10 percent of those surveyed expressed thanks or appreciation for their colleagues. Nearly two-thirds of respondents said they never express gratitude at work, and 35 percent said that their bosses "never" thanked them.[8]

Studies show that gratitude at work can increase both productivity and happiness, so when we aren't giving or receiving it, we're shortchanging both ourselves and our coworkers.

Tap into the Power of Gratitude

Whether you are dealing with a major life-shattering event, experiencing a small bump in the road, or interested in improving your relationships, gratitude can help.

"When we become more grateful, and acknowledge what we have through a lens of appreciation, it helps us focus on what is important to us," explains Louis Alloro, a senior fellow at George Mason University's Center for the Advancement of Well-being. "We are conditioned to focus on what's not working rather than to look at what is working. Gratitude changes what we look at and how we see it. It's an essential ingredient for a life well-lived."

Many people emphasize the importance of "being" grateful, but Alloro teaches it's important to take it a step further and "feel" gratitude. "It is key to feel it in your heart instead of keeping it in your mind," he says. "When you say you're grateful for something, it's very often something that happened in the past—even if it was earlier that day. So I encourage people to not just say why they're grateful, but to take a moment to remember how they felt when that was happening."

Taking time to feel that appreciation again releases dopamine and allows you to reenact the experience emotionally, generating healing positive feelings. "The payoff is huge," Louis says. "It takes a little more time and more effort, but you'll see such a difference in the way it affects you."[9]

get happy

Keep a gratitude journal. Once a week or once a day make notes about the people, things, or circumstances for which you are grateful. Your notes don't have to be long—a sentence or two is enough to remind you of the gifts you've recently experienced.

Use words that acknowledge the external source of goodness. Grateful people use words like "gifts," "givers," "blessings," "blessed," "good fortune," "fortunate," and "abundance." "In gratitude, you should not focus on how inherently good you are, but rather on the inherently good things that others have done on your behalf."[10]

Encourage gratitude. Ask your child, grandchild, or a friend, "What was the best part of your day today?"

Write a gratitude letter. Send or hand deliver a note of thanks to someone who has made a difference in your life.

Relive the feeling of gratitude. Go beyond identifying a positive experience and mentally relive it. Focus on how the experience made you feel. Savor that feeling.

You must live in the present, launch yourself on every wave, find your eternity in each moment.

—HENRY DAVID THOREAU

hat are you thinking about right now? As you look at the words on this page, what's going through your mind? Chances are your thoughts are flipping between what you're reading here and a project at work, or plans for this evening, or the vacation you wish you could take, or the things you need to add to your shopping list, or how you're going to break bad news to someone you love, or how excited you are about seeing your kids when they come home from college.

Our minds wander constantly, from one worry, plan, regret, or distraction to the next. And although *wondering* and a little intentional daydreaming is important for our curiosity and creativity, a *wandering* mind misses out on the happiness available this moment, too often because it's fearing the next.

Mindfulness, experts say, is a practice that helps us self-regulate our attention—in other words, mindfulness helps us pay attention to our thoughts. Staying mindful, or in the moment, allows us to appreciate life as it happens. When our minds are busy focusing on the present, it's impossible to also be ruminating about the past or worrying about the future. Beyond the reduction of negative thought patterns, a host of benefits can be reaped simply by staying in the moment, research reports.

"When I start talking about all the things mindfulness can do, I sound like a snake-oil salesman," jokes Richard Sears, of the Center for Clinical Mindfulness and Meditation at Union Institute and University in Cincinnati. "It increases happiness, improves relationships, helps alleviate conditions like depression and chronic pain. . . . But really, what's going on is awareness. It's about paying attention, bringing us back to what is going on right now."

Based on a twenty-six-hundred-year-old Buddhist practice, mindfulness has sparked global interest in recent years. Today, mindfulness is frequently practiced independently of any religious context. But if sitting in the lotus position doesn't sound very comfortable to you, don't worry. Although mindfulness is a form of meditation, it doesn't necessarily require chanting or sitting cross-legged on the floor. (But if a certain position or phrase helps you focus, have at it!)

"It doesn't have to be done in the same formal way as what we would normally think of as meditation," Sears explains. "Mindfulness can be taking a breath, taking a moment to notice the trees while taking a walk; it's more about setting aside time to be with yourself—in whatever form that may take."[1]

As you read the stories in this section, you'll notice that people practice mindfulness in different ways. For some, mindfulness includes traditional meditation tactics. Others forego mantras and focus on the practice as a way to *be*, moment by moment, no matter what's going on around them. Likewise, people have different purposes for engaging in the practice. Regardless of the how or why behind the practice, the common benefit that comes from staying in the moment is increased happiness, and that makes mindfulness worthy of our attention.

Gretchen Rubin

Savoring the Moment

Gretchen Rubin remembers driving from one place to another and not recalling details along the way. Another time, walking to her home office after a weekend spent taking her daughters to children's parties, she suddenly felt as if she snapped back into consciousness. "That was a very eerie experience. It was like I was back, but where had I been?" she says.

Gretchen recognized that she had a great life. She was a Yale-educated lawyer turned writer who was married to the love of her life, with two wonderful young daughters, close relationships with her family and friends, and good health. But little things perturbed her. Small setbacks were inordinately disappointing. She wasn't as happy as she could be. "I had everything I could possibly want—yet I was failing to appreciate it," she notes. "I didn't want to keep taking these days for granted."

Thus began the *rest* of her life: a series of experiments in the pursuit of happiness, which she chronicled in her blockbuster bestseller *The Happiness Project*. But although the topic she studied was happiness, the entire project as well as the books that have followed—*Happier at Home* and *Better Than Before*—have helped her live more purposefully and mindfully.

Knowing Yourself

As Gretchen threw herself into researching what made people happy, she realized she couldn't follow someone else's playbook. For example, although meditation makes many people more content, Gretchen knew sitting and focusing on a single thought wasn't for her. Over time, she identified and challenged what she calls "true" rules (rules about what is considered universally true), common ways of thinking that tended to dictate her actions and decisions without her even realizing it.

For instance, she says, "Everybody loves shopping. I hate shopping, but it took a long time to understand that about myself. Everybody loves shopping. Everybody loves crossword puzzles. Everybody loves wine. I don't love any of those things." Gretchen came to realize that mindlessly applying the "true" rules resulted in decisions that didn't necessarily support her happiness.

"It's so easy to get swept up in what we assume is true, what other people think is true. So part of mindfulness is catching yourself having these thoughts, so you can decide whether you really want to accept them," Gretchen says.

Gretchen tried other things to stimulate mindfulness. She posted sticky notes to help foster certain moods—"focused and observant" at her laptop and "quiet mind" in the bedroom, for example. She tried hypnosis (which helped), laughter yoga (which did not), and a "Drawing on the Right Side of the Brain" class (which was hard and stressful, but ultimately satisfying).

One more thing that helped Gretchen was keeping a food diary. She wanted to eat more healthfully and to lose a few pounds without going on a diet. She also wanted to stop eating the less than healthy snacks she mindlessly picked up, like low-fat cookies, individually wrapped candy, pretzels—"fake food," she calls it.

After she recorded everything she ate, she saw how much "fake food" she consumed and gave it up cold-turkey. Gretchen then realized how much this habit contributed to feelings of guilt, self-reproach, embarrassment—and that she was much happier doing without.

Noticing Negative Thoughts

Before she began work on mindfulness, Gretchen wasn't even aware of the amount of mental time she spent going over her to-do lists, worrying about what-ifs, and reliving minor grievances. Gretchen now has lots of tricks to stop the negative thoughts: go to sleep if it's near your bedtime, listen to a zippy song, hug your child, pet an animal, check an entertaining website. "But the problem with rumination is even realizing that you're ruminating. It's the constant practice of mindfulness—of just noticing what's going on in your head—so you can say, 'Oh my gosh, why am I allowing myself to be in this downward spiral?' and then stop it."

Gretchen admits she tends to have a temper, but mindfulness has helped. "I just behave myself much better now, because I'm more aware of things that are taxing me, like if I am hungry, too hot, or didn't get enough sleep. The more aware I am of myself, the more I have forbearance or understanding for other people's points of view. I have a long way to go, but I do behave myself much better."

Although she's constantly sharing what she's learning through her books, blogs, and podcasts, Gretchen says she doesn't preach to her family. Or at least not since her sister good-naturedly called her a "happiness bully." But she's seen them pick things up. "When I'm calmer, they're calmer. When I'm thoughtful, they're thoughtful."

She's not there yet, though. "Mindfulness—I just think it's so, so important. You'd think it would be so easy—just hang out with yourself all day. But it's the great challenge of our lives, and everything else flows from it."

HAPPY ACT
Break the Rules

What do you do on a regular basis simply because
"everyone" likes it? If you don't like it, stop doing it!
Carve your own path to happiness.

Adam Shell

Pursuing Happiness

When Adam Shell decided to make a documentary about happiness, it wasn't because he wanted to be happier. Nor did he consider himself an expert on happiness. In fact, when he and his coproducer, Nicholas Kraft, began interviewing happiness experts, they quickly realized how little they knew about the one thing everyone wants most.

His goal for the film *Pursuing Happiness* was to change America's culture. "Culture is the stories we tell about ourselves," Adam says. It bothered him to know that the United States is ranked twenty-third on the UN's list of happiest countries in the world. He believes the problem, at least in part, is that the media predominately report bad news. "Is that going to make us a better society? I'm not saying [the news] is not important, but we need to be telling equal or more stories about the things we're doing right, the things that make us thrive, and things that give us reasons to live and be happy and help and support other communities." So Adam set out to tell better, happier stories.

He'd first gotten a taste of what uplifting, real-life stories could do for people when he directed a seventy-minute film about the talent agent and pop-culture art collector Richard Kraft (and Nicholas Kraft's dad). The central theme of the film was: fill your life with what makes you happy. Intended for a one-time showing at Richard's birthday party, *Finding Kraftland* ended up playing at film festivals across the nation and even won a Best Documentary award at the 2007 Central Florida Film Festival. Person after person who had seen the film told Adam it had made them think about what they could do to bring joy into their lives.

"When you do something that inspires people to be happier, there's nothing like that," Adam says. "I wanted to have that feeling again."

Happy People Everywhere

During the next few years the idea of creating a film that layered relevant science from happiness experts alongside interviews with ordinary, happy people began to take shape. Things really got started when he sent an e-mail to twenty friends asking: Who is the happiest person you know? "People's recommendations came in a flood. Everybody wanted to be involved," he says. Adam and Nicholas set up interviews and began filming in 2012, and in 2013 they hit the road in search of complete strangers to interview.

"We wanted to tell a bunch of stories about people who were doing it right," Adam says. "It was never a problem for us to find them. We could literally walk into a café and get a referral from the waiter." And each person they met along the way taught them a little more about happiness—what it means, how to find it, and why living in the moment is the only way to really experience it.

One of the people they interviewed was Gloria, a twenty-eight-year-old corporate attorney and self-described "hip-hop DJ vegan farmer" who was diagnosed with stage IV colon cancer. She personified for Adam the idea that mindfulness shapes the way people experience life. "She said, 'I'm not going to let this be the worst thing that happens to me. In fact, I'm going to make it the best,'" Adam remembers. Others in similar circumstances might have given up or sunk into despair, but Gloria danced through cancer treatments, made time for laughing with friends and family, worked in her garden, and started a nonprofit. "I want to be one-tenth as strong as her," Adam says.

Prior to her diagnosis, Gloria thought a lot about the future—she made career plans and reminded herself that her time and effort would pay off in the long run. Her future-focused perspective ended when she was told she had a disease with a 10 percent survival rate. "Every day is an experience to get excited about and to be looking forward to. I'm looking forward to the next minute," she told Adam and Nicholas. "So I have this very high level of satisfaction with my day; it's hard to have peaks and valleys."

In an interview with life coach Gary Van Warmerdam, they learned why Gloria's in-the-moment approach to life brought her so much happiness despite tragic circumstances. "Happiness is fundamentally an expression," Gary explained. "What you're putting out there you're experiencing as you put it out there."

"That's one of the moments that hits me most in our film," Adam says. "If I say, 'I love you,' I feel love. If I say, 'I hate you,' I feel hate. If I smile at someone, I experience a smile; it doesn't matter if they smile back at me. That was really powerful to me. Something so simple, but I'd never thought of it before." He also notes that it takes conscious effort to respond to each moment with love and gratitude, regardless of one's circumstances.

"Mindfulness is a practice of just being aware—aware of yourself and your surroundings, your reactions," Adam says. "So many of us go through life so disconnected from ourselves. This is what causes people to be stressed out and unhealthy. I am definitely more cognizant now that I have a choice in every moment about how I'm going to act or react. For me, the biggest thing that I've taken away from this is the understanding that there is a way to get from sad to happy. I've seen people do it."

Adam intended to create a film that would change the way society views happiness. And maybe it will. Regardless of what the project does for other people, Adam knows his life will always be a little happier.

HAPPY ACT

Smile

Smile at strangers today. Pay attention to how you
feel when you share a genuine smile with someone.

Barb Schmidt

On Becoming Mindful

There was a time Barb Schmidt did not know you were supposed to be happy. That seems like lifetimes ago for the woman who is now known as a "transformational" leader by those who follow her work integrating spiritual practice with daily life.

But it was not always this way. Barb started out in a much darker place. As the oldest child of two alcoholic parents, she took on the role of protecting her four younger siblings. The notion of being happy and carefree barely crossed her mind. She had no friends and remembers her childhood as largely defined by loneliness.

As soon as Barb turned sixteen, she left home. As a manager at Mc-Donald's, where she had worked since she was fourteen, she earned $165 a week. With that money, she was able to get her own apartment and buy a small car. That initial independence was only the beginning of the success she would experience. More important, it marked the start of her significant personal transformation.

By age twenty-eight, Barb had hit the big time. She was the owner of multiple McDonald's franchises and her grim childhood was, for all intents and purposes, long behind her. She writes in her book *The Practice*: "According to society's measurements, I had achieved all the external things I could possibly want: six franchises, a handsome husband, a social life, money, and an attractive appearance too. However, despite my obvious outward success, I did not feel happy. Most of the time I felt incomplete. 'Is this what happiness is?' I wondered."

Listening Inward and Living in the Present

Doubts continued to nag at Barb, made worse by her struggle with bulimia. It was only when she finally sought treatment for her eating disorder that her real life's work began. In the rehab center, Barb was introduced to meditation. She also began practicing a twelve-step program and started devouring inspirational reading—Deepak Chopra, Marianne Williamson, Thich Nhat Hanh.

She sold her franchises, cofounded Ronald McDonald Children's Charities of South Florida, and dedicated herself to living mindfully. Key to her work in mindfulness was practicing a morning meditation—which calmed her mind, dispelled distractions, and taught her "to listen inwardly."

"With a consistent meditation practice we truly start remaking ourselves from the inside out . . . embodying Gandhi's message of peace: anger transforms into compassion, hatred into love, impatience into patience, and insecurity into security," she says.

Another ingredient in Barb's recipe for mindfulness is what she calls "living present." She uses a meaningful word or phrase—a sacred mantra—to help her maintain that inner peace and focus on the now throughout the day. "Living present" is a concerted effort to quit living through the mind alone—thinking about the barrage of to-dos, recriminations, speculation, self-doubts—and focus on what is happening in the moment at hand. Constant practice has helped Barb learn how to focus on more positive qualities like gratitude or compassion and train her mind to go where she directs it. "[Reciting your sacred mantra] intercepts or slows down the rush of thoughts, helping you to act mindfully rather than mindlessly react," she says. Like many others who practice mindfulness, she's discovered that reciting a mantra helps chase away negativity, reduces stress, quiets the radio noise of life, and generally reinforces the inner calm achieved through meditation.

There are other elements in Barb's mindfulness journey, such as daily reflection and letting go of the past, that have helped her find the happiness she desired. "Each day, little by little, through sitting with myself every morning, I began to connect to the place inside that is loving, strong, and complete. Over time, I felt an overwhelming sense that all is well with my life and the world around me. By loving and accepting myself, I experienced a beautiful sense of connectedness to all beings and life. It has to start this way; we can never find happiness and love without being able to give to ourselves first. My spiritual path has awakened me to this truth," she says.

Still, the path to mindfulness requires practice. Barb is disciplined in her daily meditation and in doing the work to let go of what doesn't matter, so she can live fully in the present. She says it is this daily mindfulness work that has redefined her understanding of happiness.

"Happiness is not something fleeting as in, 'I'm happy today because this went right, but I'm unhappy tomorrow because this went wrong,'" she says. "We are not at the mercy of the happenings in the external world. I live my life from 'the inside out,' so my happiness is not an up-and-down emotion, but rather comes from a deep sense of contentment and peace. Happiness means I am strong, loving, capable, and complete in this moment. Not only will I survive when life sends me difficulties; I will thrive."

Today, Barb is an attractive fifty-something philanthropist and teacher and is happily remarried. She started a program at Florida Atlantic University in 2003 as a platform for her interest in mindfulness and peace and brought in speakers, such as the Dalai Lama and Jane Goodall. That program morphed into her book, which describes the tools she's used to manage stress, find inner peace, and uncover happiness. And in 2011 she founded an international nonprofit, Peaceful Life, Peaceful World, to help others live happier, more fulfilling lives.

Barb has come a long way from the sad little girl who had no idea life could be full and rich and brimming with joy. But after experiencing such a life, she wants to spread the word: happiness is possible.

HAPPY ACT

Take Five

If meditation is new to you, sitting still for
thirty minutes or an hour many seem impossible.
Start small. Take five minutes to sit quietly.
Tune out the world around you and focus on a
single, grateful thought.

Alanis Morissette

Ever Mindful

Alanis Morissette's smile is infectious. She glides through the world in a peaceful dance, guided by an innate sensitivity. "I'm very focused on that intrapersonal intelligence—cultivating the interiority," she says. Grounded, living in the moment, Alanis finds stillness in a chaotic world. "I stay mindful when the schedule is hectic. For me mindfulness is about being present and hypersensual. That means feeling the breeze on my skin."

Alanis's focus is really about getting as much as she can out of life. She begins with communication with the self, a journey inward. Then her spiritual side helps her connect with something larger than herself, providing a sense of purpose and gratitude. It involves "cultivating that sense of oneness, that sense of interconnectivity, of being inextricably linked with all beings."

Then there's her family, social groups, teachers, and people who've influenced her. "I'm obsessed with rendering each relationship as functional as possible. And mindfulness is a mandatory prerequisite for that," she says. "When I listen to someone who's speaking to me, my shoulders are pointed toward them, I have eye contact. I'm listening and not attempting to interrupt. Basically, I'm listening as well as possible; it's not always possible, but when I can, I consider myself to be a very blank slate."

Massive success came early to Alanis. At the age of nineteen, she introduced *Jagged Little Pill* to the world. Catapulted almost immediately into fame, she suddenly had millions of passionate, loyal fans and back-to-back sold-out concerts. She traveled week after week on an eighteen-month worldwide tour. The fans couldn't get enough of Alanis. "After *Jagged Little Pill* there was nowhere for me to go physically where I wasn't recognized, whether it was to the grocery store or a hotel," she says. "You know, I couldn't go anywhere where I could return to that sense of just being that happy little brown-haired girl from Canada."

She credits traveling to India as a joyful moment in her life after being burned out from the endless touring and huge success. "I think I was only recognized maybe four times, on the train. . . . I was just going into temples and meditating, sitting still for sometimes four and five hours in a row." During and after her trip to India, she found a sense of stillness. After learning about mindfulness meditation in India, Alanis went on to create more music, win awards, and sell millions of albums. However, what she learned there stuck with her—she learned to turn inward. She calls it "one giant mindfulness meditation trip."

The happiest experience of Alanis's life was giving birth to her son, Ever Imre, in 2010. She describes it as a "pretty blissed-out, oxytocin-riddled moment." To her, raising a child is about being as attentive as possible: "I just think mindfulness and parenting are the same thing. If we're distracted or we're barely there, we're technically not parenting." Alanis built a studio in her Los Angeles home, so she could raise her child mindfully while also working on her passion and career.

Loving by Being Present

"For me, offering presence is commensurate to offering love," she says. "Offering that to a child is the greatest gift of all." For her, being a parent is akin to activism, in the sense that you're making the world a better place by bringing new life into it. "It creates the foundation of what this planet will evolve into," she says.

Her husband, Mario "Souleye" Treadway, a fellow musician, joins her in choosing a mindful path—for parenting and all aspects of life. They met at a meditation gathering. "He came with a mutual friend of ours, and when he walked in I just thought, 'Wow!'" Alanis says. It stood out to her that he was "oriented toward really doing the brave inner work, the kind of inner work that isn't always comfortable." After all, she says "practicing mindfulness is easy when circumstances are pleasant and enjoyable. Mindfulness gets a little more challenging when what we are asked to be mindful about is painful, or unpleasant, or anxiety-inducing. This is when the practice's rubber really hits the road: to bring presence to each feeling that comes up in a given circumstance. To inquire into this feeling is not to 'get rid of it,' but to allow it its moment in the sun, allow its message to really get through to us. Feelings, when really understood, often have profound messages for us."

Alanis has weaved mindfulness throughout her life, especially when creating music. "I can't write a song unless I'm 100 percent present," she says. "I'll say, 'Okay, I'm going into the studio this afternoon from one to four. I'll take breaks, and during those breaks I'll check texts and be accountable to other people, but while I'm writing, the door is closed and the 100 percent intention is to focus on the song coming through.'" Her attention is on just the moment of creation, the moment when the song comes through her and onto the paper.

Regarding goals for happiness, Alanis says, "There is a version of happiness that is a oneness with what is. It's a quality of peace. If our egos are going to chase anything, that would be the lovely thing to chase." And if anyone has caught it, it's Alanis.

HAPPY ACT
Focus on the Person in Front of You

Today, practice paying complete attention to whomever you happen to be with. Actively listen. Notice the other person's body language. Not only will your full attention help you connect with the other person; you'll make that person feel important.

The Science Behind the
Wisdom of Mindfulness

"In Asian languages, the word for 'mind' and the word for 'heart' are the same. So if you're not hearing mindfulness in some deep way as heartfulness, you're not really understanding it. Compassion and kindness toward oneself are intrinsically woven into it. You could think of mindfulness as wise and affectionate attention,"[2] says Jon Kabat-Zinn, who began studying the effects of mindfulness in the 1970s at the University of Massachusetts Medical School. His work, including the Mindfulness Based Stress Reduction (MBSR) program, which was the first documented structured program to teach mindfulness, became the model for many programs developed since then. Today, MBSR programs have been implemented in more than two hundred medical centers, clinics, and hospitals around the world.

Neuroscientists continue to investigate how mindfulness can change both the structure and function of our brains, and psychologists use it for their own cognitive improvement as well as to help clients with everything from anxiety and depression to compassion and self-acceptance. But mindfulness has gone far beyond the medical and wellness communities. In the marketplace business leaders are looking at how mindful decision making can redefine their workplace, and educators are embracing such concepts as mindful learning and mindful reading. Studies also show that mindfulness can improve communication and happiness between couples and coworkers. The practice has even been used in prisons to help reduce hostility and mood disturbances among prisoners.

Becoming Aware

Richard Sears, author of *Mindfulness,* works in the area of Mindfulness Based Cognitive Therapy (MBCT), a form of MBSR that also uses cognitive therapy–based exercises. Cognitive therapy explores and challenges negative thought processes. MBCT is effective in treating problems like depression and anxiety, he says, because it creates a connection between our thoughts and our feelings.

"Once you've experienced depression, it cuts a pathway in your brain and makes it easier to become depressed the next time you feel sad," Sears says. "MBCT teaches you to notice signs of the problems coming up, so you can prevent them."

Mindfulness teaches us to take a moment, take a breath, and get back to what is happening right now rather than reacting to the what-ifs of the situation. The practice can keep a rough patch in your day from spiraling into negative thoughts that trigger bad memories and depression.

"With more awareness comes better choices," Sears says. "If I'm aware of how I'm reacting, I can lower my stress response, and that makes other things better. I'm less vulnerable, my immune system can heal better. Everything improves when you become more aware."

Healthier Mind, Healthier Body

The mind-body connection has been well proven over time, and mindfulness proponents and practitioners say it holds many keys to creating a healthier, happier life by positively influencing the body. "It's not a cure-all, but it will assist in whatever a person is struggling with, whether that's physical, mental, or emotional," says Ryan M. Niemiec, education director at the VIA Institute on Character and author of *Mindfulness and Character Strengths.* "It offers support and assistance in whatever you're trying to accomplish. Take, for example, someone with chronic pain; to learn how to face that directly is a huge challenge. But to bring an honest awareness to your own suffering can completely change your relationship with it."

"Before" and "after" brain scans show that certain areas of the brain develop new neural connections after practicing mindfulness for about eight weeks. Richard Sears equates these physical changes in the brain to building muscle by lifting weights—over time, you get stronger, but it has to be maintained in order for the results to continue.

Some clinical studies have focused on how mindfulness can influence specific ailments, including substance abuse, anxiety, PTSD, depression, autism, cancer, multiple sclerosis, heart disease, AIDS, high blood pressure, and headaches. On the broadest level, mindfulness is seen as a tool to improve health, because it boosts our immune system. Scientists explain that, when practiced regularly, mindfulness can lead to lower secretions of cortisol and adrenaline, hormones that suppress the immune system.

Driven to Distraction

A study by the National Science Foundation discovered that, on any given day, our brain generates some fifty thousand thoughts. That averages out to about fifty-two thoughts a minute during waking hours, so is it any wonder that many of us find it a challenge to "stay in the moment"?

As a doctoral student at Harvard, Matt Killingsworth became interested in the association between happiness and what we're thinking about. He developed the Track Your Happiness app to study the causes of happiness and monitored users in real time. With more than 15,000 subjects in over 80 countries, Killingsworth collected 650,000 "live" reports that led to the conclusion that "a wandering mind is an unhappy mind." People who were "in the moment" consistently were happier than those whose minds were wandering, even if they were performing a task they didn't enjoy.

What Killingsworth found most surprising was just how often our minds wander. Overall, our minds are on something other than what we're doing 47 percent of the time. And, unfortunately, when our minds wander, they usually aren't visiting a happy place. We often end up with anxiety and worry about the future or anger or regret about the past. Killingsworth's studies showed that a wandering mind isn't the consequence of unhappiness and related anger or anxiety; it's the cause of it.

"The only moment we can ever be in is the present," Sears points out. "Mindfulness is about being in the moment, bringing our attention back to what's happening right now." For most of us, learning to be in the moment takes some work, because we have to undo what's become a deeply ingrained pattern. As children, we have the innate ability to enjoy the present moment as it unfolds, but before long we're taught to start thinking about the future. "We're often taught that the 'good thing' is coming. It's always about the next thing," he says. "Over time, we lose the capacity to enjoy good moments. Even when we [accomplish] a great thing, we're already thinking about what's next."

There is a place for planning, he says, but the current model doesn't allow us the chance to enjoy the moment. As children, we start talking about what we'll be when we grow up; we go to high school and think about college, and while in college we dream of the career that's waiting for us. The cycle continues once we get that job; we start saving for our dream house, working for the next promotion, building the future. Before long, it's time to save for retirement and plan for the golden years.

"About middle age, a lot of us wake up and realize we've been tricked. We realize, 'This is my life! It's not coming; it's already here!'" Sears says.

Putting Mindfulness into Practice

Mindfulness can help put us back in touch with our true thoughts and feelings, and millions of people around the world have found it transformational. One of the most effective paths is through meditation, but Niemiec says many people are intimidated by the idea.

"The three most common reasons for people to abandon their mindfulness meditation practice is that their mind wanders, they forget to do it, or they don't have time," Niemiec says. "Meditation is a way of cultivating mindfulness, so having a formal meditation process is helpful in improving that. But it's more about finding the right fit."

For one person, that fit might be a centering prayer; for another it might be self-hypnosis; someone else might choose to do insight meditation. Many classes and online courses now exist to teach mindfulness and meditation practices.

Keep in mind that there's no one-size-fits-all solution; it's what works for the individual. Rather than sitting quietly, for example, some people prefer to take mindful walks as a way to improve positive emotions. Instead of allowing thoughts to roam, those on a mindful walk would notice the breeze, the feel of their shoes hitting the ground with every step, and the sounds of nature or the city around them.

Walking and eating mindfully are easy, effective ways to take a break—and they can be done unnoticed by others. Here are some other simple, common ways to implement mindfulness:

Sit quietly and observe what you're experiencing in that moment. Observe the sights, sounds, and smells that typically go unnoticed during a busy day.

Take note of the physical sensations you're feeling, whether it's the texture of a book in your hands, the feeling of the chair against your legs and back, or the feeling of water splashing on your skin as you wash your hands.

When experiencing anxiety, depression, or anger, become an observer. Look at how your body is responding to the emotion instead of becoming absorbed in the feeling itself. Ronald D. Siegel, of Harvard Medical School, likens this particular form of mindfulness to watching clouds drift by; Jon Kabat-Zinn compares it to watching soap bubbles float in the air. Try using the experience as an opportunity to understand the feeling rather than reacting to it.

And when all else fails, just take a breath. "With mindfulness, there is no goal other than to become more aware," Siegel says. "A great place to start is just to breathe. Follow your breath. It's something we all have. And you'll notice physiological changes almost immediately."[3]

get happy

Take a breath. Breathe in deeply through your nose. Feel the air come into your body and fill your lungs and diaphragm. Hold your breath for a beat, and then exhale slowly, noticing how it feels when the air leaves your body.

Take a bite. Pay attention to the food in your mouth—the texture and flavor. Chew slowly. Enjoy the taste.

Take a moment to be aware of your body. From head to toe, notice how you feel—from the inside out. Notice any tension and consciously relax those muscles.

Focus on the moment. Practice doing one thing at a time. Give your full attention to the task at hand.

HEALTH

You know, all that really matters is that the people you love are happy and healthy. Everything else is just sprinkles on the sundae.

—PAUL WALKER

For more than twenty years, Marge Jetton kept a Friday morning appointment to have her hair styled. She met her regular hairdresser in Loma Linda, California, at eight o'clock sharp, and went through the same routine—the rollers, the football helmet–shaped dryer, the feather-soft pages of *Reader's Digest* to flip through, and of course the easy conversation.

Marge had a routine before her appointment too. She performed a morning devotional, walked a mile, lifted weights, and ate her usual oatmeal before climbing behind the wheel of her root beer–colored Cadillac Seville and setting out for the day. On the particular Friday that Marge was joined by longevity researcher Dan Buettner for this ritual, she was counting the days to her 101st birthday. Marge was born on September 29, 1904.

Marge's busy day didn't end with a trip to the beauty shop, of course. After the hair appointment that Friday morning, she took Buettner along for her regular volunteer work. Her compassion for others was part of the reason she felt a purpose in carrying on. Marge had lost her husband in 2003, two days shy of their seventy-seventh anniversary. "It took me a year to realize that the world wasn't going to come to me. That's when I started volunteering again. . . . I found that when you are depressed, that's when you do something for somebody else."

Buettner recounts his meeting with Marge in his 2008 bestseller *The Blue Zones*. "I don't know why God gave me the privilege of living so long," she told him. Buettner's research shows that Marge's longevity may have had much more to do with science than divine providence. The daily lifestyle Marge modeled—one similar to those of the other centenarians living in what Buettner dubbed "blue zones," the areas with the highest concentration of people age one hundred or older—simply lends itself to a long, happy, meaningful existence. The author has devoted his career to studying centenarian-rich pockets in Japan, Mexico, Costa Rica, Italy, Greece, and southern California.

"You have a certain awe for someone who has reached triple digits," Buettner says. "When you spend enough time with them, you discover a uniformity—they tend to have a sense of humor. They tend to listen. The grumps are kind of weeded out before age one hundred."[1]

Buettner's research matches up with findings from other longevity studies. On their own, a clean diet, positive outlook, regular activity, and meaningful relationships can each contribute to greater life satisfaction. Combine them the way Marge and the other blue-zone centenarians have, and you have a recipe for not only an impressively long life, but also one filled with happiness.

In this section, you'll read about people who are taking strides toward healthier living. And in the final section of this chapter, we'll share insights that may help you adopt some of these good-health practices yourself. What we hope you'll see is that living a healthy life isn't about looking a certain way; it's an investment you make in yourself, so you can share your best with the world.

Tory Johnson

A Shift for Good

"Lose weight, or lose your job."

Those weren't the words Tory Johnson's boss said when she smoothly suggested a stylist and perhaps a little exercise—but they were the words Tory heard.

She knew she didn't need to lose just ten or fifteen pounds to improve the way she looked during her "Deals and Steals" segment on *Good Morning America*. She needed to drop at least fifty—more would be better, since the camera didn't do her any favors.

She left that fateful meeting holding back the tears until she was safely home and locked in the bathroom and thought about how many times she'd tried to lose weight. The struggle with the scale had been going on for almost four decades. After so many futile attempts at shedding the extra pounds, she says, "Failure, time and again, led me to be resigned that this is just the way I am, even though I didn't like it."

In so many aspects, her life was good, but her weight had long been a source of unhappiness. "Society is very quick to say happiness shouldn't be defined by a number on a scale or a dress size. And that's true. But being overweight brought a lot of frustration into my life," Tory says. "I've always been very happy in my marriage. I have two incredible kids, who are a source of happiness. I have a phenomenal career, and I am blessed to get paid to do what I love very single day. Family, career . . .

when you look in those buckets, they are filled with genuine happiness. But then there's another bucket of health and wellness that wasn't remotely happy, because I felt I was trapped in a body I didn't like."

That unhappiness about her body "trapped" her in fear whenever an invitation came for a party or wedding. "I was immediately thinking, 'How can I get out of this?' because I didn't wear dresses," she says. Trying on clothes at the store felt like a special kind of torture to be avoided at all costs. She also refused to go to the doctor—for ten years—because she didn't want to hear a lecture about her weight. Losing a job she loved because of her weight was a trap in which she refused to be caught, however. That fear turned out to be the spark Tory needed to make a permanent shift in her life.

Adopting a New, Healthier Lifestyle

"Diets are a temporary pause in bad behavior. I needed a permanent change," she says. Those changes, of course, included making healthier food choices, but she knew her weight challenges were really more about what she believed than what she consumed. "It's not about what we eat; anyone who needs to lose weight knows what not to eat. Most people fail because of something that needs to change in their minds. I realized that what I put in my head was more important than what I put in my mouth."

So in addition to choosing foods that were actually good for her and noticing when she was full, she gave up believing that she was destined to be overweight. "I reminded myself that this is the one thing that is totally within my control," she says. "For so long, I had put forth so much negative energy around avoiding losing weight as opposed to changing things. I would try to convince myself that everyone has something they're unhappy about, and I would think, 'I have a really great family and friends, so what if I'm overweight?' But there's nothing good about having to make excuses."

Tired of failed quick fixes and diet fads, Tory committed to changing her life, bite by bite. One strategy that helped her stay focused was to intentionally test each craving with the question, "Is this my preference or my priority?" "Potato chips are my preference. But my priority is my health. And my priority is going to trump my preference. By pausing and thinking 'Preference or priority?' I made the right choice. And every time I made the right choice, I felt better about myself. Eventually, I started to see results."

Another strategy that helped was giving herself what she calls the "luxury of time." "I didn't give myself a deadline. I had faith that I would eventually [lose the weight]." And she did. Within a year, she dropped sixty-two pounds.

"If you would have told me on day one, 'You're going to lose sixty-two pounds over the next year—about a pound a week—and you're going to give up the foods you love, and you're going to exercise,' I would have said, 'No! A pound a week? That's torture!'"

But not having a deadline made her goal seem a bit less overwhelming. "On day one a year looks like an eternity. But looking back, it always feels as though it flew by; in retrospect a year passes so quickly. When we give ourselves the luxury of time and benefit from that time by maximizing it and staying focused and determined, we can accomplish incredible things. And a year is a solid amount of time to do something amazing."

It's been a few years since that meeting her with boss. Tory has kept off the weight, and even dropped a few more pounds. She's been to the doctor and no longer minds trying on clothes—a good thing since she needed a whole new wardrobe. It feels good, she says, to look back and see how far she's come, and not just in terms of weight loss. "There's something powerful about being able to make changes and seeing things through. It's a source of deep pride that brings great happiness."

HAPPY ACT
Make One Positive Choice

What small step toward a big goal can you take today?

Arianna Huffington

Everything Can Wait

Finally she slept. But this was not the restorative snooze Arianna Huffington had hoped to slip into during the early hours of April 6, 2007, following a workaholic bender. This was sleep the hard way. The bloody way.

Arianna, who was then attempting to power her toddler-age news site and blog *The Huffington Post* through sheer personal force, had given way to exhaustion. The eighteen-hour workdays finally caught up to her. As she collapsed in her office, her head crashed against her desk on the way to the ground, breaking her cheekbone.

By most measures, the media magnate was an American success story, a Greek immigrant who had rebounded from divorce a decade earlier to become virtually a household name in her mid-fifties. But very few people who wake up in a pool of their own blood feel great about themselves. "I was not living a successful life by any sane definition," she writes in her 2014 book, *Thrive*.

Arianna realized that the ghastly scare in her office was a clear sign that she needed to change. In the years since, she has taken better care of herself by managing her stress and sleep and never forgetting to seek joy. She has devoted herself to helping the people close to her find health and peace as well. And because of this, rather than despite it, she argues, *The Huffington Post* has grown to unimaginable heights. Arianna sold the site to AOL in 2011 for $315 million and cut a deal to remain on hand as the leader. *HuffPo* was valued at as much as $1 billion by tech insiders following AOL's sale to Verizon in March 2015.[2]

A month after the AOL-Verizon deal, she explained the nuts and bolts of her powerful personal transformation in a *SUCCESS* magazine cover story. At first, Arianna recalled, she needed to learn to ask the right questions about her life. What is living well? What steps must be taken to achieve it? "If you think about it, success in the beginning was really about having a good life. 'What is a good life?' the philosophers would ask. And then we shrunk it down to these two metrics—money and power. And that's really shrinking the definition of what it means to be human."

Recharging, One Decision at a Time

Following her wake-up call, Arianna at first made incremental changes. In *Thrive* she describes easing slowly from four hours of sleep a night to eight, enjoying along the way the newfound peace and energy that she carried with her all day. So too came perseverance and resilience in the face of each day's challenges, and in turn stress began to slip away. The gentle shifts in her focus and energy led to living in the moment—to enjoying the distinct textural burst of a blueberry or the crispness of a clean bedsheet. And she found a new appreciation for the people in her life. She saw the business managers, editors, and writers at *HuffPo* making the same mistakes she had made and realized that she should use her painful experience to advise her leadership.

Arianna believed that what was good for those who worked for her would ultimately be good for *The Huffington Post*. The idea that to be successful a company needed its executives to work 24/7, she realized, was out of date—and just plain wrong.

To keep her employees refreshed, Arianna, in 2011, opened a pair of napping rooms that are now a hallmark of the *HuffPo* offices. Rather than guzzle more coffee or energy drinks, employees are encouraged to take an on-the-clock siesta. Weekly yoga, meditation, and breathing classes followed. Healthy snacks abound. "It's really a culture," Arianna told *SUCCESS*. "We are trying to make sure that everyone knows that after work they're not expected to answer e-mail, for example. . . . Everything can wait; they can unplug and recharge themselves."

Arianna's *Thrive* mantra has spread beyond the workplace where she presides and the pages of the book that explained her story. It is now one of the cornerstones of *The Huffington Post*. Right alongside the usual categories like politics, business, and entertainment sits Healthy Living, encompassing topics like "GPS for the Soul," "Moments, Not Milestones," and "Stronger Together." A two-inch headline one recent evening proclaimed "5 Big Benefits of Being a Doodler."

And maybe the doodling thing is exemplary of the *really* big lesson that Arianna learned through her ordeal—to not take work quite so seriously. She actually credits her mother with teaching her as a girl that "angels fly because they take themselves lightly."

As Arianna wrote in a post on her site, "Whenever we find ourselves in a stop-the-world-I-want-to-get-off mind-set, we can remember that there is another way and open ourselves to grace. And it often starts with taking a moment to be grateful for this day, for being alive—for anything."

When we are grateful for *anything*, Arianna reasons, we'll take much better care of ourselves, so we can experience more of it. And there is so much to be experienced!

HAPPY ACT
Shut It Down

Work can wait. Really. When you leave the office,
silence your phone and turn off your computer.
Give yourself the gift of a little downtime every day.

Natalie Wilgoren

One Step at a Time

With her sixtieth birthday rapidly approaching, Natalie Wilgoren wanted to do something different to celebrate the occasion. No cake, no party. She wanted to run. One foot in front of the other, as far as she could possibly go.

Natalie lives in the seaside town of Boca Raton, Florida, where she works as a psychiatric nurse practitioner helping people who suffer from mental illnesses. In her thirties, she'd taken up running briefly, but she'd always start out too fast or too hard and burn out.

Through her forties and fifties, she stayed active with lower-impact activities, usually indoors, like using an elliptical machine and doing strength training at the gym. Although she'd always considered herself a relatively positive person, as sixty loomed, she felt as though she was missing something in life. "It wasn't that I was unhappy, but in retrospect I could have been happier," she says. "And I was active, but not as active as I really wanted to be."

She was also twenty pounds overweight and felt constantly tired and sluggish. Her doctor warned her about her high blood pressure and high cholesterol. "I knew I needed to make some lifestyle changes," she says. "I just didn't know exactly how to do it."

Just as her sixtieth birthday was closing in, the answer to her question came in the mail. She'd been receiving flyers from Team Challenge, an endurance-training program that raises money for the Crohn's and Colitis Foundation. Several people in Natalie's family suffer from Crohn's disease, so the pamphlets triggered something within her: she could help change other people's lives while also improving her own.

Running for a Cause

So on a whim she signed up for the Team Challenge Rock 'n' Roll Half Marathon. Running 13.1 miles would be the farthest she'd ever gone on foot. As part of her training, she'd also raise money for a cause she believed in. She started by walking, then slowly worked up to a jog. She ran from one lamppost to the next, and each time she was able to run a little bit farther. None of it was easy.

"I definitely had physical limitations. It would hurt, but I would just keep doing it," she says. "Soon I got addicted."

Natalie joined a running group, and they'd meet every Saturday morning at six for a long run. "It was a big commitment," she says. "I had to force myself to go to bed early, so I could wake up early." But somehow, instead of feeling tired, she found herself energized. "I don't need to rest as much," she says. "If I run in the morning, I have more energy and I'm more focused throughout the day."

It didn't take a very long run to boost her energy. Even logging a couple of miles, at a pace barely faster than a walk, provided positive effects, like the confidence-boosting shot of endorphins some call a "runner's high."

The Rock 'n' Roll Half Marathon in Las Vegas takes place each November. Some twenty-seven thousand people show up to run up and down South Las Vegas Boulevard, (a.k.a. The Strip) and be cheered on by the bands playing at each mile marker. At the starting line of the half marathon, sixty-year-old Natalie stood there in her running shorts, waiting anxiously for the starting bell. It was cold out, and she'd come from balmy Florida, but that didn't matter. She felt charged and ready. The buzz in the air, generated from a street packed with runners, made her feel more alive than she'd felt in years.

She walked much of that first race, but what mattered most is that she crossed the finish line—and then went on to pass countless more finish lines. She signed up for 5-kilometer races, 10-kilometer races, and a handful more half marathons, each time pushing harder and faster. Through her running, she raised money for research on Crohn's disease and colitis as well as breast cancer. Each race gave her a goal to work toward and focus on.

For Natalie, running turned into a destination sport. Races along the coast in Boston, on Washington's Olympic Peninsula, and in Savannah, Georgia, gave her motivation to travel and run someplace new. She encouraged her family and friends to join her on a few of those races too, pulling people into the sport that had transfixed her.

The running group she joined, hosted by her local running store, turned into her best motivation and a great social outlet. After the runs, they'd all go out for a well-earned breakfast and laugh over omelets and coffee. "There's a group of women, and we're all at the same pace," Natalie says. "On runs, we wait for each other, we look out for each other."

The more she ran, the more weight she lost, and she started feeling stronger and sleeping better. She felt more confident and more content with all aspects of her life. "My life felt more balanced, between work, friends, and my health. Plus, it all felt like a big accomplishment," she says. "And that made me happier."

Now sixty-five, Natalie doesn't run quite as often or far as she used to, but she still loves the way it makes her feel. Getting up early in the early-morning light and running still makes her happy, as does sharing the benefits of running with her patients, who struggle with depression and anxiety.

"I've read a lot about the benefits of exercise in reducing anxiety. But instead of telling them to go and start running, what I often do is tell people to start by going for a walk," Natalie says. "I tell them, 'You can do anything for a short amount of time and build on it.' Once they get moving, I've noticed subtle changes. Accomplishing small goals makes people feel more self-assured. I know that to be true because I've seen it myself."

HAPPY ACT
Take a Step Toward Health

You don't have to run a marathon—just start walking or jogging. Celebrate when you reach a new milestone, even if it's only that light at the end of your street.

Roy Rowan

Ninety-Five Years Young

If you asked Roy Rowan what he does to stay not just alive, but active, engaged, and mentally sharp at age ninety-five, he would simply say, "Keep doing what you love to do." He learned a long time ago that the key to keeping the brain healthy with age is to always be trying something new to challenge himself and shake up his routine. And so he has. The catch here is that what Roy loves to do may sound more like a one-way ticket to an early grave than a prescription for longevity.

After graduating from Dartmouth in 1942, Roy joined the Merchant Marines to combine his writing and photography talents with his love for the sea. Shortly thereafter, he was drafted into the army to serve in World War II. His first assignment was escorting Italian prisoners of war out of North Africa under fire from Mussolini's troops. From there, Roy was sent on combat loading missions to various ports in Asia just prior to the Hiroshima and Nagasaki bombings. Roy's experience in the army set him on a trajectory of adventure that has yet to end.

"By the end of the war, I had fallen in love with Asia," Roy explains. World War II had ended, but the Chinese Civil War was still raging. Roy took a job with the United Nations running trucks distributing food and clothing to Chinese civilians within the war zones until a bullet hit his windshield and he decided it was time to take a break and go home.

Craving a Life of Adventure

During his time in China, Roy wrote stories about and took photographs of the conflict and sent them back to magazines in the United States. At a chance meeting in a Shanghai hotel bar, Roy had encountered Bill Gray, the city's bureau chief for *Life* magazine, and learned that they were about to publish some of his photos. Once Roy returned to the States, Bill urged *Life* to hire him as a correspondent, and thus began a mentorship and friendship that continued throughout Roy's career. Back he went to China and Southeast Asia. He was on the front lines of all of the major battles leading up to the fall of Shanghai—and he enjoyed every minute. "When you're in danger and under fire, you just crave more excitement," Roy explains nonchalantly.

That kind of passion and enthusiasm has continued well into his later years. Roy has published ten books since he "retired" from his last magazine job in 1985 and tells everyone, "You don't have to turn in your computer at sixty-five. If you don't use your mind, you'll lose it." Even when he wasn't pursuing controversial stories for *Life, Time, Fortune,* or *People,* Roy rose early, worked out often, and did the *New York Times* crossword puzzle religiously, at least the first half of the week: "Monday and Tuesday I could manage, but I never got far once I started the Wednesday puzzle," he laughs about the famous grid that gets progressively harder as the week goes on.

Learning new languages is another way to build up your gray matter, and Roy took advantage of that opportunity while in China. "I learned to speak phonetic Chinese to communicate. I couldn't read or write it, but I could understand and speak it," he recalls. "And I am especially good at swearing in Chinese!"

A key reason Roy was able to keep up this pace was the support of his wife of sixty-one years. After his return to the States in the early 1950s, he was introduced to two women. The first, whom he was urged to date by his friend and mentor Bill, was Helen Rounds, a photo researcher for *Life,* and the second was a Broadway starlet by the name of June Lockhart, who would soon become a TV star and household name. Intrigued by both women and unable to make up his mind, Roy decided he wasn't the type to settle down and took an assignment in Germany. A few months later, he realized his mistake when he heard Helen was seeing someone else.

"I called her and told her to come to Germany and marry me the next week. I was very forceful, but I still can't believe she did it," he says with awe. If following your passions is longevity secret number one, his marriage proved to be secret number two. "Helen was peaceful, calm, loving; she was the yin to my yang," Roy recalls of his soul mate, who passed away two years ago. "The toughest part of our marriage was my need for adventure. We had very few disagreements, but one in particular was when she objected to my going to spend a month with Jimmy Hoffa for an article for *Life* magazine. She though it was way too dangerous. But when I insisted, she accepted it, and gave me her full support," Roy recalls. Together they raised four sons, all of whom remain close to their father. Roy has not been without health challenges. He has battled three forms of cancer: melanoma, prostate, and bone. His first cancer diagnosis—of melanoma—was back in 1974, when he was covering Vietnam. Roy had to have immediate radical surgery that took six hours, which no one was sure he would survive. Forty years ago, most people didn't survive any form of cancer, let alone one as serious as melanoma. Roy, however, wasn't about to give in. He spent his time in the hospital writing a six-thousand-word article for the *Atlantic* on the connection between a positive attitude and a strong immune system. The cancer went into remission and never came back.

During his recovery from melanoma, he took up a rigorous walking program of five miles a day. He then progressed to running, an activity Roy continued until he was eighty-five. Roy still exercises regularly, usually by riding a stationary bike.

Roy's sons—a marine biologist, a photographer, an English teacher in the Ukraine, and an oilman in Texas—all share his love of adventure.

"Growing up in an adventurous family has led my sons to take more chances and bigger career risks in their lives," he says. And the adventure continues. His oldest son, Marc, is taking Roy on a trip to the Amazon in November, one of the few places in the world he hasn't seen. "Marc actually called up my doctor and asked if it was okay for me to go," Roy says, "and he pronounced me in good health. I tried to get some friends to come along, but they're all too old and not up to it," he chuckles mischievously.

HAPPY ACT

Tease Your Brain

Puzzles are fun and just might be an excellent way to keep your brain sharp. Sudoku, jigsaw, crossword . . . Pick your favorite and start solving.

The Science Behind the
Wisdom of Health

Health and happiness are intertwined in a way that science can't fully explain. It's sometimes difficult to determine which comes first. Are people happier because they're healthy, or do happy people experience better physical and mental health? The answer to both questions seems to be *yes*.

What science can definitively tell us is that people who practice healthy habits, such as exercising and eating well, enjoy a wide range of benefits, including:

Better sleep: One study found that people who exercised at least twenty minutes a day reported 65 percent better sleep quality.[3]

Better concentration: Exercise stimulates blood flow, which can help you feel more alert and focused.

Fewer colds: Regular aerobic exercise (moderate activity five times a week) has been shown to increase immunity against bacteria and viruses.[4]

A longer life: One study found that even fifteen minutes of daily exercise could increase a person's life span by three years.[5]

Other studies have credited healthy living to a better sex life, a happier disposition, and reduced risk for depression, migraines, and cardiovascular disease.

Get Moving!

The long list of benefits that come with regular exercise is hard to ignore. So why is it so difficult to get up and get moving? Busyness is one of the most common, reasonable-sounding excuses for not exercising. But it turns out that physically active people tend to have more energy and be *more* productive than those who sit at their desks all day. Then there's the excuse that you don't have time to take care of yourself, because you have to care for everybody else. Another fib. Self-care, including exercise, refuels the body and mind and equips us to be better caregivers.

Some people avoid exercise because they think it's too hard or they've yet to find an activity they really enjoy. Let's be real. Not many people like the idea of sweating in front of strangers or spending hours comparing themselves to svelte or muscular gym goers. But exercise doesn't have to be a miserable, humiliating experience—nor does it have to be confined to a gym. In fact, you're far more likely to be motivated to get active on a regular basis if you actually *enjoy* the activity.

"One key is the realization that reaping the benefits of physical activity is not just about sweat," explains Michelle Segar in her book *No Sweat*. "An almost infinite variety of physical movement choice and intensities will work just as well as, or better than, a strict regimen of intense workouts— especially when people have chosen activities they actually enjoy doing." A behavioral sustainability researcher and self-care coach, Segar encourages clients to get started by simply moving. "Take any and every opportunity to move, in any way possible, at whatever speed you like, for any amount of time. Do what makes you feel good and stop doing what makes you feel bad."[6]

Dr. John Ratey, an associate professor of psychiatry at Harvard and author of the book *Spark,* explains why exercise and happiness go hand in hand. Although it may take a while before you notice lower numbers on the scale, he says anyone who exercises can enjoy immediate benefits. "People talk a lot about endorphins that are released through exercise, but that is just part of it. When we begin exercising, we almost immediately begin releasing dopamine, norepinephrine, and serotonin. Those are all neurotransmitters that deal with feelings of reward, alertness, contentment, and well-being."

Even more important, the brain begins to secrete something known as brain-derived neurotrophic factor (BDNF), a protein that is associated with the growth and development of neurons within the brain. Ratey calls BDNF "brain fertilizer," noting that it has been proven effective in combating both depression and anxiety and has even been successful in fighting substance abuse issues. "In general, it allows us to combat stress hormones directly within the body, but also to combat outside stresses overall. And all of those things contribute to our feelings of happiness."[7]

Maybe you, like Natalie Wilgoren, enjoy running. Great. Lace up and get out there. But if you loathe running, don't force it. Go for a walk, ride your bike, or take up ballroom or salsa dancing—alone or with a buddy. Just get moving.

Change Your Diet, Change Your Mind

Live Happy science editor Paula Felps explains that another key factor in both the quantity and quality of life is the food that we eat. In today's world of prepackaged choices and fast-food options, we've gotten far away from the wholesome, nutritious foods that our bodies need to function healthily and happily. And that processed diet is not only wreaking havoc on our bodies; it is also negatively impacting our mental health.

Most conversations about the evils of processed food focus on what it's doing to our waistlines. The Western diet certainly isn't doing us any favors in that department, leading to skyrocketing obesity rates, but it's also having just as significant an impact on how we think, feel, and function.

The Center for Mind-Body Medicine, in Washington, D.C., believes so strongly in the connection between good food and good health that it offers "Food as Medicine" training programs to health-care professionals including medical doctors, chiropractors, nurse practitioners, physical therapists, and psychologists. Dr. Drew Ramsey, who serves on the board of the center and is an assistant clinical professor of psychotherapy at Columbia University, also uses food as treatment for many of the mental-health issues, including anxiety and depression, that he sees in his practice. "All of the molecules that end up in your brain start as food," Dr. Ramsey says. "So we need to appreciate the fact that nutrients like omega-3 fats play a role in helping brain disorders and [improving] our mental state."[8]

Eating the right foods can change your mood, enhance your memory, and even affect conditions like attention-deficit disorder. And getting rid of the wrong foods can have just as amazing an effect. Eliminating foods with added sugar, for example, can not only help you shave off a few pounds and decrease the risk of heart disease, diabetes, and high blood pressure; doing so has also been linked to less depression and greater mental alertness. Many of the dyes, artificial flavorings, and fillers used in today's processed foods have negative effects on us, both physically and emotionally, and could be creating what Dr. Ramsey refers to as "false moods." In other words, you really don't feel as bad as you think you do!

In fact, a 2010 study in the *American Journal of Psychiatry* showed that women who ate a standard Western diet of processed and fried foods, refined grains, and sugars showed much higher levels of depression than research subjects who ate diets rich in plant foods.[9] That study echoed the results of research findings published a year earlier in the *British Journal of Psychiatry,* which showed that those who ate foods like desserts, fried food, processed meats, refined grains, and high-fat dairy products were one and half times more likely to suffer from depression than those who ate a diet consisting mainly of vegetables, fruit, and fish.[10]

Research indicates that up to one half of all depressed patients are found to be deficient in the B-complex vitamin folate, which is found in foods like lentils, asparagus, black beans, spinach, and broccoli. Low levels of vitamin D (found in eggs yolks, mushrooms, and fatty fish like tuna and salmon) have been linked to suicide, and a deficiency in omega-3 (found in seafood) "is a risk factor in suicide, major psychiatric disorders, personality disorders, despair, homicide and suboptimal social cohesion," says Phil Domenico, a research scientist and consultant for the health and wellness industry.[11]

Simple shifts to more wholesome, less processed foods can change your energy and your mind. Beans, nuts, eggs, and kale are among the natural choices that will rejuvenate your body while feeding your brain.

The great news is, the better you feel, both mentally and physically, the more you'll enjoy your life. And studies we've cited throughout this book help explain why happy people live longer—and stay healthier—than their less cheerful counterparts. Happy people have lower incidences of stroke, coronary heart disease, cancer, and disability later in life. Interestingly enough, happy people are even less likely to die in car accidents.

So whether you're eating and exercising to be happy or healthy, getting active and choosing the right foods can allow you to do both. And best of all, they will let you enjoy that healthy, happy life even longer.

get happy

Do what you enjoy. You don't have to "hit the gym" to get healthy. Go for a bike ride. Take a dancing class. Walk to the park with your kids or grandkids—and don't just sit on the bench. Swing, play catch, and, even if everyone's looking, try out the slide.

Catch some zzzzz's. Sleep allows the body to reboot. Go to bed a little earlier today and see how you feel after a few extra hours of sleep.

Choose brain foods. Beans, nuts, eggs, and kale are all great options.

Find a buddy. Having someone join you in an effort to live healthier gives you some accountability and can add to the fun.

RESILIENCE

No matter how far life pushes you down,
no matter how much you hurt,
you can always bounce back.

—SHERYL SWOOPES

*T*he young woman answered the ringing phone and heard a stranger's voice on the other end of the line.

"Do you want to know where your husband is?"

In a matter of seconds, her contented life was turned upside down. The stranger gave her an address where she could find her husband and told her that he had been having an affair. After calling a friend to come watch her little one, she drove to the address the mystery caller had given her and found her husband's car parked in the driveway.

In the following weeks and months, her plans for a white-picket-fence future fell apart. After a tearful confrontation and a few too-late counseling sessions, it was clear that her marriage was over. Her husband moved out and left her with a pile of debt and a baby on her hip. Heartbroken, she wanted to climb into bed—and stay there.

But she didn't. Instead, she wiped away her tears, went back to school, and created a vibrant life for herself. The end of her marriage, as terrible as it was, offered a chance for a new, brighter beginning. She discovered for the first (but not the last) time that she was strong, smart, and capable enough to handle whatever challenges life brought her.

That ability to bounce back is known as *resilience*. It's a character trait that, like a muscle, can be strengthened with use. When researchers study resiliency, they look for at least two distinct identifiers. The first is a stressful or traumatic disruption of life. It could be the death of a loved one, a work crisis, an unwanted divorce, an automobile accident, a medical diagnosis, or any number of other tragic events. Whatever the cause, the disruption rips you out of your normal existence and throws you into emergency mode.

There, with jagged pieces of shattered dreams at your feet, you have the opportunity to take the second, crucial step toward recovery. It is with this step that resiliency is exercised. You see, it isn't simply survival that defines resilience; it's the ability to learn and grow from the experience—to become better equipped to handle life's challenges and perhaps even happier because of a newfound personal strength or perspective toward life.

In the inspiring stories that follow, you'll read about people who have bounced back after life-threatening circumstances, crises, and personal loss. Today, these people use their resiliency skills to help others thrive. Their lives demonstrate that, regardless of the tragedy that befalls you, it is possible to find your way into a vibrant and valuable existence. To be certain, your life may never be the same; you may always feel a sense of loss. But as you build resiliency, you just may discover that you're stronger than you ever imagined.

Rhonda Cornum

Soldiering On

Dr. Rhonda Cornum recognizes that most people remember her for "one week of misadventure." But what she learned from that week—and what she has been able to teach others as a result—is where her real story lies.

Rhonda was a thirty-six-year-old army flight surgeon in 1991, when her Black Hawk helicopter was sent to rescue a downed F-16 pilot. During the rescue mission, her helicopter was shot down, and Rhonda—who broke both arms, injured her leg, and was shot in the back—became an Iraqi prisoner of war.

"I don't recommend [being a prisoner of war], but it is better than being dead," says Rhonda, now a retired brigadier general. Despite the grim reality of her situation, she instinctively knew she had to look at the bright side to get through her ordeal. "I knew always to look at how bad it *could* be, not how bad it was," she says. And, given that the alternative was death, "it didn't look so bad to be a prisoner."

She was interrogated by her captors, but when she failed to provide the information they wanted, they dragged her outside, where she was reunited with another survivor of the crash, and then surrounded by a group of soldiers who put guns to her head.

"I'm kneeling there, trying diligently to think of something positive," she recalls. She thought about the fact that her daughter, who was thirteen at the time, would grow up and become successful. She thought about the wonderful life she was grateful to have enjoyed so far and that, at the very least, this end to her life would be quick and painless.

It turned out to be a mock execution, something designed to make her more forthcoming with information and, as she learned later, a common tactic used on captured soldiers. It was also, she says, "the single most anxiety-producing event I experienced while I was there."

At that point, she realized she had one job ahead of her: to stay alive until she could be rescued. "The ability to change your mission in midstream because you have to is a good skill. It's something everyone should learn."

Over the next few days, that adaptability was crucial. Keeping a positive attitude and reining in her thoughts kept her going, despite the fact that she didn't know when she would be rescued. She never let herself entertain the idea that she wouldn't make it out alive; instead, she focused on the positive. It's a resilience she says was genetically ingrained in her, but it also takes practice, determination, and conscious choice to follow that path.

"Attitude is key," she says. "Sometimes that's the only thing you have left. They can break your bones, they can deprive you of sleep, but they can't determine what you think. You have to keep your mind from wandering into a bad place and then staying there."

When she was released eight days later along with twenty-three other prisoners of war, Rhonda says she "came out a better person." She'd had the chance to practice, in an extreme situation, the mental discipline that she knew was so valuable in maintaining a positive attitude. She had seen firsthand the importance of not letting her thoughts go to a dark place, and once she had been rescued, she used those same techniques to keep from ruminating on her captivity.

Instead of focusing on what had gone wrong, she was grateful for what she had learned from the experience and for the strength it reinforced within her. Her resilience may have surprised others, but it was something she expected from herself.

"Resilience allows you to be successful, even when things are not going well," she says. "Happiness is a word that means so many things to different people. For me, it's not just that I'm laughing or smiling. It's that I feel gratitude and my life has meaning and purpose."

Taking a Proactive Approach to Resilience

Her experiences and revelations about resilience led her to become the first director of the army's Comprehensive Soldier Fitness Program. Launched in 2008, the program is designed to boost psychological strength by teaching soldiers resilience.

"There's no doubt that everyone can learn it," she says. "It's like learning to play tennis. It doesn't mean everyone is going to get really good at it, but some training is always better than nothing at all. If you don't have good training, you're going to be less effective."

Teaching soldiers resilience skills before they enter potentially traumatic situations is the psychological equivalent of teaching them weaponry before sending them to a war zone. The approach upended the previous mentality of only finding and treating psychological and emotional injuries after the fact. It's a tactic she thinks should become more prevalent and not just for soldiers.

"You need to learn that kind of thinking before [the event], when you can practice. When it doesn't work, you can try again. You would never send a guy to war and expect him to learn how to sight and load his weapon while someone is shooting at him."

Soldiers who are trained to deal with the emotional and psychological challenges of war are also often able to change the outcome of harrowing circumstances. Follow-up reports show that soldiers who were given resilience training before being deployed returned with fewer substance-abuse and anger issues. "We're making better people, and better people make better soldiers."

Her takeaway from seeing the results of resilience training is that everyone can learn to both handle negative situations more effectively and recover from trauma more quickly when given the proper tools. Today, Rhonda splits her time between raising dogs in Kentucky and serving as director of health strategy for TechWerks Healthcare IT Solutions. TechWerks offers science-based resilience courses for real-world situations, with courses tailored specifically for military and first responders as well as for workplaces. The company also is working with the South Australian Health and Medical Research Institute's Well-being and Resilience Centre to improve well-being for the state, where she's seen its training lead to positive changes in the lives of people ranging from children to the elderly.

Mental agility, maintaining a positive attitude, practicing gratitude, and learning to control one's thoughts while facing very real threats are all skills that can be developed. And, she says, "These skills work just as well whether you're a soldier, a farmer, or a student. These skills make you more empathetic, make you a better communicator."

And, regardless of whether you're a POW or a Ph.D., Rhonda says resilience is a life skill that everyone can benefit from. "Resilience can get you through anything," she says.

HAPPY ACT
Minimize Catastrophic Thinking

If you're facing a challenge and feel yourself caught in a downward spiral of worst-case thinking, stop and focus on best possible and most likely outcomes. Once you've identified the most likely outcome, develop a plan to cope with that eventuality.

Sabriye Tenberken

The Beauty of Blindness

She can still picture one of the last beautiful things she saw with her own eyes. She was sitting by a dam in Andorra, Spain, her gaze fixed on the lake in front of her. Her mother pointed out the way the light danced on the water.

Sabriye Tenberken is forty-four now, but the reflection of light on water—on a lake, on a river, on waves—remains fixed in her memory. It is something her parents made a point of showing her when she was a child growing up in her native Germany—the visual magnificence of the world around her. What they chose not to tell her, at least initially, was that degenerative retinal disease would eventually make it impossible for her to see any of it.

The choice her parents made—to seek the positive, instead of being consumed by the negative—is reflected in Sabriye's attitude toward the loss of her sight at age twelve. Her parents wanted to save her from the dread of living in darkness. They knew they could not stop her from going blind, but they could help her collect many beautiful, visual memories and prevent her from spending the rest of her sighted childhood in fear.

And they did, for the most part. By the time Sabriye understood what was happening, things moved fast. She had only a short period of frightened anticipation of darkness. Blindness came, but she quickly learned she didn't have to be afraid of the dark.

She did, of course, spend a period feeling sorry for herself. Then she made a conscious decision to treat her blindness not as a disability, but as an asset, "something very, very beautiful." Sabriye discovered that lack of sight heightened her other senses, and she focused on the things she could do now that she wasn't able to do as well before. Without visual distractions, she found she could concentrate better. At the same time, necessity forced her to be an expert problem solver and communicator. Lacking visual input, she began to imagine her surroundings in a more beautiful and colorful way. "All of these experiences," she explained, "can make you happy."

Seeing Past Adversity

Instead of feeling bad when she experienced discrimination and roadblocks, she made it her mission to change things. When she wanted to study Tibetan, which at the time did not have a Braille script, she created one. She was twenty-two. It took her two weeks to develop what would become the official writing system for the blind in Tibet. When she wanted to get involved in humanitarian work but was told by established organizations that her blindness would prevent her from working in developing countries, she created her own organizations—a school for blind children in Tibet and an entrepreneurial training program in southern India for people who have overcome adversity.

"And that's a happiness too, to have an understanding that you have meaning in life and this is your battle, this is what you are going to change," Sabriye said. "This is something that at least makes me happy. And I do see it with the kids as well."

"The kids" are those she works with at the Tibetan school for blind children. Graduates of the school can speak English, Chinese, and Tibetan. After the intense three-year program, they are integrated back into mainstream schools. Several are now studying at college. Others have established businesses and families. Sabriye's positive outlook on life and impressive ability to make the best out of every situation is reflected in students like Gyurmi, now applying for college. When Gyurmi was a boy at the school, Sabriye and several colleagues once came across him grinning from ear to ear.

"Why are you so happy?" they asked him.

"I am so happy, because I am blind," he replied.

It was a startling answer for a boy living in a country where the blind have long been shunned due to a belief that blindness is a punishment for the wrongs of past lives. They asked him to explain.

"I am the only one in my family who can read and write, and I'm the only one in my village who can speak three languages fluently: English, Chinese, and Tibetan. And I'm the only one in my whole region who can work on the Internet," he told them. "And all despite the fact, actually because of the fact, I am blind."

Sabriye and her life partner, Paul Kronenberg, a social engineer from the Netherlands, have expanded this teaching—that adversity creates opportunity—at the kanthari institute they cofounded in southern India. The institute is a training ground for innovators who happen to be former child soldiers, albinos, and "disabled" individuals. Students are chosen not out of charity for a perceived hardship, but because their ability to overcome adversity is viewed as an asset that enables them to help others.

It is this same positive, empowering attitude that has governed every part of Sabriye's life. Instead of focusing on the difficulty of getting around in developing countries where there are no beeping streetlights and signs in Braille, she points out the abundance of nonvisual indicators, like strong smells. Then there are the human interactions she depends on in these situations: the driver she trusts to take the correct payment from her purse, the hand of a street child leading her to her destination. The street children are a particular favorite; she feels a solidarity with them, a bond.

What others might see as a bad thing, Sabriye sees as something to be cherished. Blindness is not a disability, she explains, but "a different life quality."

HAPPY ACT
Look at Your Problems Differently

Look for one potential positive outcome.
A single ray of light may be enough to fill you
with the courage to keep going.

Lauren and Mark Greutman

Thriving After a Financial Crisis

Nine years ago, new parents Mark and Lauren Greutman started digging a financial hole. They fell in love with North Carolina while on vacation and decided to move there—never mind that Lauren's thriving business was supported by clients in their hometown of Syracuse, New York. They'd experienced some career success in their young lives and felt their efforts deserved a few rewards, like a brand-new home. Not just any house, but a 3,600-square-foot custom home. They picked out every doorknob and detail of the home and filled it with expensive new furniture. And every cent, except the hefty mortgage loan, went on credit cards.

The cherries on the sundae were Lauren's Cadillac and Mark's brand-new Audi A6 "with leather seats and automatic everything," Mark remembers. "That was one of the first luxury items we bought. I admit it was fun driving it around."

The couple assumed that their lifestyle and spending were common for people their age who had achieved a measure of professional success. But it didn't take long for them to realize their dream life was not what they'd expected. "We were so dumb with money," Lauren says now. "We were also so focused on things that we lost sight of what was important to us."

Lauren had taken on the role of handling the family's finances, and as such she made most of the credit-card purchases. But not long after arriving in North Carolina, the business she'd started in New York dried up. As an actuary, Mark received a good salary, but it was not enough to cover their monthly expenses. Credit-card bills piled up, and the family operated at a deficit of $1,000 per month. "I kept these facts from my husband," Lauren says. Though they had always been close, those secrets weighed heavily on her and created stress in their marriage.

But as the debt mounted and it eventually became impossible to make ends meet, Lauren came clean. "I laid out all the cards on our bed, and for the first time we added up all our debt," she says. They were sick to learn the sum came to $40,000. "I was scared Mark would feel betrayed or angry. But he hugged me and said he forgave me, and we committed to working it out."

"It was hard news to hear. It wasn't completely unexpected, though," Mark says. "I kind of knew what was going on, but was way too passive to confront it. I just secretly hoped it would turn around."

The next day Lauren got a job as a waitress at a steakhouse, working six nights per week. After being a business owner for several years, she says, "It was very humbling."

The credit-card debt was not the end of it. One day soon after Lauren revealed the extent of their debt to Mark, she watched through the blinds of her enormous master suite as a tow truck hauled away her Cadillac. Ten teenage boys on skateboards grabbed the bumper and trailed the car down the street. A few weeks later, the couple received a notice from the IRS announcing they were being audited and that they owed the government $17,000.

Sacrificing for a New Way of Life

"I finally came to terms with the fact that that part of my life was over," Lauren says. Living with one car, working opposite schedules, and raising a young son became too stressful. They realized they spent $1,000 monthly on food and figured that if they cut their food spending to $200 monthly they could afford for Lauren to quit the restaurant and stay home. The family got serious about a budget, cut out every single extra thing they could think of—cable, vacations—and began couponing in earnest.

In 2009, at the height of the nation's financial crisis, the Greutmans qualified for a short sale on their house. They sold almost all their furniture, including a drum set of Mark's, who was a lifelong drummer. "Selling my drums was a symbolic way of saying that I was willing to sacrifice to get a handle on our finances," he says. Free of their possessions and high overhead, the family, which now included a new baby, moved back to Syracuse and into an 800-square-foot townhouse.

In 2009, Lauren started a blog to teach others about couponing and budgeting, IamThatLady.com, with the idea that she might earn $300 monthly from ad sales and brand partnerships to help pay for tuition for her kids to attend a private school. Any income above that sum went toward paying off debt. The blog took off and spawned what has since become a six-figure business teaching others how to get out of debt.

It took the Greutmans three years of frugal living to become debt free. Their determination paid off, and they've learned from their mistakes. For example, when Lauren and Mark, who now have four children, bought their new home, they made sure the mortgage for their $96,000 house was well within their budget. Despite the increased demands on their finances, they are committed to living on $5,000 per month, even though their digital business grosses much more. "We consider luxuries to be things like giving to our church, sending the kids to private school, putting money aside for our children's college education, and a retirement plan that allows us to quit working when we want," Lauren says.

Their new lifestyle has made them a happier couple, says Mark. "Learning to communicate about our finances has made us so much closer," he says. They've also learned that creating a financial plan together provides them with an incredible sense of freedom. Lauren likens their budget to a protective barrier rather than a restriction. "It's as if you lived near a freeway. You wouldn't let your kids play in the yard without putting a big fence around your property. Money is like that: with bound-aries, we don't have to always worry about it, but we still have money to spend."

HAPPY ACT
Come Clean with Yourself

Ignoring problems often allows them to grow—
especially if the problem is a result of your own
mistakes. Admitting your mistakes may not be easy,
but it will allow you to create a plan of action,
so you can recover.

Celeste Peterson

Always a Mom

Celeste Peterson raised her only child for eighteen years and eight months—and was grateful for every minute. "Being Erin's mother was my job, my passion; it was something I wouldn't trade for anything," she says. She relished watching Erin become a tall, outgoing young woman with dreams as wide as her smile. Erin's dream job was to help people by working for a nonprofit, Celeste says. She hoped to travel overseas and adopt orphans. "Every day with her was exciting. I always described it as a gift."

On April 16, 2007, that gift was snatched away by a student at Virginia Tech, who killed thirty-two schoolmates and faculty before turning his gun on himself. Erin was among many believed to have died instantly, shot in the head during French class.

In the following weeks, there were times Celeste wished she were dead too. The future she had so looked forward to—helping Erin through the challenges of dating, working, marrying, raising kids—wasn't going to happen now. At home in Centreville, Virginia, Celeste rarely ventured outside. Unable to face her coworkers at the aerospace and defense company where she works as an administrator, she holed up in her office and avoided the cafeteria.

Soon, though, she started getting signs it was time to rejoin the world. First, donations poured in from all over the country in Erin's name—

unsolicited. Celeste and her husband, Grafton, set up the nonprofit Erin Peterson Fund and dedicated those gifts to providing college scholarships to promising high-school students and supporting other worthy projects. Then a friend invited Celeste to Westfield High School, Erin's alma mater, for a meeting of a new leadership group for at-risk boys. The friend told Celeste she thought that helping this group was in her "wheelhouse."

"At the time, not a damn thing was in my wheelhouse," Celeste recalls. "I felt like saying, 'Can't I just sit in a corner? Can't I just cry? Why are you pushing me? I can't help people! I can't even help myself!' But I guess some people know you better than you know yourself."

Mending a Broken Heart by Helping Others

Celeste went to the meeting. She doesn't remember it well—about twenty-five kids were listening to a speaker of some kind—but she vividly recalls what happened as it ended. One of the boys in the group came up to Celeste and told her that Erin had been his friend. She had urged him to "stay out of trouble" and would escort him from one class to the next to make sure he didn't ditch. One time, he said, Erin pulled him away from a fight by his collar. At that point, Celeste says she "kind of caught the fire." She gave the Boys' Leadership Group $3,000 from the Erin Peterson Fund and started helping to plan social and educational events for the boys.

"I knew that what I was really good at was being a mother . . . and I felt like my skills were not being put to good use after Erin had passed." Celeste, a devout Christian, has no doubt that Erin was helping from beyond the grave to find her an outlet for those skills. "It just seemed like I was getting evidence all the time from her that I needed to keep doing what I did best."

The more Celeste worked with the boys at Westfield High, the more she found herself becoming the glass-half-full person she used to be. She was smiling again, laughing, saying hello. Volunteering through the Boys' Leadership Group "gave me a purpose," she says. "The kids, just being involved with them, they made me feel connected. They made me sharp, they kept me relevant, they just kept me going."

Other pursuits—cooking, riding her bike, and listening to music— helped Celeste recover. As did keeping a journal about her feelings, including some she felt ashamed to admit out loud. After Erin's death, Celeste described in her journal how seeing other parents celebrate their kids' achievements sometimes made her hate their happiness. "All of the stuff you have inside of you you're able to pour out into a journal, and you're better," Celeste says. "Sometimes in pouring it out on the page, you start crying, but you know it's cathartic, because you feel so much better afterward."

A few months after Erin died, Celeste began seeing a therapist who helped her realize she needed a little mothering herself. "She hugged me, and I just remember melting into this stranger's arms. It felt so good. . . . What a therapist does is she gives you the tools to cope. It's somebody there you can talk to who can help you walk through this thing."

Celeste's loved ones have stuck by her as well—further convincing her that to bounce back from a tragedy, you can't isolate yourself. "I tell people all the time, if it wasn't for my friends, my neighborhood, my church, I don't know how I would have made it." Highest on her list of supporters is Grafton, to whom she has been married thirty years. "The only person who understands my pain is him," she says. "We talk about Erin all the time."

Celeste still cries for her daughter, she says. "Every day I'm challenged to figure out how I'm going to live in this world, happy but never knowing joy." When she feels that way, she's got to "look to Erin and what her expectations would have been for us." And then Celeste gets busy again, using her maternal gifts.

So far, the Erin Peterson Fund has provided at least $76,000 in college scholarships and $73,000 in grants. Almost all the grant money has gone to the Boys' Leadership Group, giving the students experiences that would be hard for their families to afford. Celeste and company have taken them on field trips (colleges, Hershey Park, theaters); brought in inspiring speakers (athletes, businesspeople); and treated them to the occasional country club meal, preceded by a lesson in table etiquette. "My goal is the same goal I had for Erin—anything I can do for you, I do," she says.

One day, Celeste believes, she and her daughter will be reunited in heaven. But she doesn't need to wait till then, she says, to know how Erin feels about the volunteer work Celeste is doing.

"I can hear her now telling me, 'Good job. Good job, Mom.'"

HAPPY ACT

Help Someone Today

In the darkest times, helping someone else
can provide comfort and a sense a purpose.
Who can you help today?

The Science Behind the
Wisdom of Resilience

In *Stronger,* George S. Everly Jr., Douglas A. Strouse, and Dennis K. Mc-Cormack compare humans undergoing stress and experiencing resilience to a rubber ball:

> In order to make it bounce back, you must put it under great pressure. The greater the pressure, the higher the ball will bounce back. Now to be clear, it's not the pressure itself that causes the ball to bounce, but the construction and attributes of the ball under pressure. It's what the ball is made of that really matters. The pressure serves as a catalyst for the rebound.[1]

You are like that rubber ball. Your character and attributes—your mental and emotional construction—determine how quickly and easily you will bounce back when challenges apply pressure to your life. And, yes, you can bounce back. Research on resiliency concludes that each person has an innate capacity for resiliency, *a self-righting tendency.* This capacity operates best when you have resiliency-building conditions in your life,[2] but *everyone,* even those who grew up with hardships or who have dealt with prolonged or recurring stress, can harness their ability to bounce back.

Cincinnati's VIA Institute on Character says each and every person possess twenty-four character strengths, the building blocks of resilience, to some degree. But it's our "signature strengths" that form the cornerstone of our personal storehouses of resilience, says Ryan Niemiec, a psychologist and the institute's education director.

For example, people endowed with lots of perseverance "generally don't see obstacles as obstacles," he says. "They see these as opportunities . . . to learn . . . to rise to the occasion or . . . to make the end goal that much more sweet." Where some people prefer to rely on hope as they focus on the future and remain optimistic through the difficult times, others draw on bravery or depend on their creativity to brainstorm solutions to challenges.

Because of the complexity of its interaction with our other personality traits, Niemiec prefers to call resilience "positive adaptation." "This means that when a stressor occurs, [resilient people] don't cower away," he says. "They also don't turn to alcohol and drugs to avoid it. Instead, they adapt in a way that is constructive and beneficial."

Ann S. Masten has dubbed this type of adaptation "ordinary magic." The University of Minnesota professor studied youth growing up in disadvantaged environments and concluded that most, despite the obstacles they faced, turned out fine. Her unexpected findings convinced her and other experts that resilience is the practical ability to combine skills such as problem solving and self-control with caring relationships and social resources to recover from setbacks.

Skills and Resources to Build Greater Resilience

Researchers have found that certain internal and external "protective factors" contribute to the development of resiliency, including strong social connections, problem-solving skills, a sense of personal identity and control over one's life, and a positive attitude.[3] It's important to note that you have significant control over many of these factors—particularly when it comes to how you think about others, your circumstances, and yourself.

By preparing now and building or acquiring these protective factors, you'll be better equipped to bounce back when challenges arise. But start now; don't wait until the crisis hits to prepare.

Finding Strength in Numbers

External factors begin with childhood and include attention given during infancy, access to caregivers at home, consistent structure and rules during the teenage years, family cohesion, and an intergenerational network of friends, which may include teachers and grandparents as well as peers.

Regardless of your age, positive relationships can be invaluable in the process of recovering from a crisis. Sometimes you'll need a sounding board—a friend, parent, spouse, minister, mentor, therapist, or personal coach. Participating in support groups can also provide a sense of solidarity with people who have been or are dealing with a similar challenge— whether it is an illness, an addiction, the loss of a loved one, or coping with another form of trauma. Having someone positive to talk to who will listen to and encourage you can strengthen your resilience.

Other times, you may discover that you need someone whom you can help. Getting involved in others' lives through volunteering in your community or church or even simple acts of kindness toward friends or strangers may provide a temporary mental escape from your worries or sorrow. At the same time, by helping and encouraging others, you may gain a new perspective—a reminder that life isn't all bad, nor is it all about you.

Maintaining Control of Your Attitude

Some of the other happiness practices discussed in this book may help you develop resilience. For example, a positive attitude or sense of optimism is extremely beneficial for resilience. The reason is that for life to get better, you must first believe that "getting better" is possible. One strategy that can help improve your outlook is to remind yourself of other challenges you've already faced and overcome. Thinking about or writing down what you've learned about yourself from previous, difficult experiences, for example, how you've grown or what you've accomplished since, or perhaps even because of, a life crisis will empower you with belief that you *can* triumph in the face of adversity.

The ability to manage your thoughts and feelings is also a part of developing resilience. Rhonda Cornum drew on this skill when she focused on what she was grateful for while a gun was pointed at her head. Even in that high-anxiety moment, she understood that she had the power to choose what to dwell on. You have that same power.

Learning to manage emotions and choose your thoughts through techniques such as yoga or meditation or by practicing mindfulness will empower you to maintain the perspective that you can survive or overcome. With your emotions in check, you'll also be better able devise a plan of action and take steps to heal and move forward with your life.

Tapping into "Post-Traumatic Growth"

Surviving any traumatic or difficult experience provides an opportunity for what experts call "post-traumatic growth"—an experience or knowledge that affirms one's own strength and ability to handle adversity. Case in point: Drs. Steven M. Southwick and Dennis S. Charney, authors of *Resilience,* found that 93 percent of the thirty former Vietnam prisoners of war they studied attributed their greater appreciation of life to being imprisoned. The POWs took a painful experience and made it meaningful by using it to readjust their priorities and self-perceptions. By doing this, they had internalized the belief: "I've been through the absolute worst, and though I'm vulnerable, I'm also much stronger than I ever imagined."

The Vietnam POWs weren't alone. Shannon Polly, who has facilitated resilience training for more than a thousand U.S. Army sergeants, says "Soldiers in World War II felt that surviving combat made them more resilient. Resilience is believing that you can learn through failure."[4]

Learn, Grow, Thrive

Most of us will experience some sort of trauma or serious adversity in our lives, and most of us will discover unexpected courage and strength in the recovery process. That's why resilience is called "ordinary magic"; it's an ability each of us possesses. Even so, it is a choice that must be made, moment by moment, day by day, until recovery is complete. And although you may forever carry a scar—some pain, like the loss of a child, may never completely heal—it is possible to rejoin life, create a "new normal," and even learn to thrive.

get happy

List your wins. What have you already overcome in your life? Looking back will remind you of how strong you are.

Choose your thoughts. Rather than dwell on worst-case scenarios, focus your thoughts on what you can control in the moment.

Give yourself some grace. Sometimes bouncing back looks more like baby steps. It may be necessary to allow yourself some time to grieve. Be patient with the healing process.

Don't go it alone. Find someone to talk to, whether that person is a professional or a friend with a listening ear.

SPIRITUALITY

Faith consists in believing when it is beyond the power of reason to believe.

—VOLTAIRE

When Lionel Richie wrote the song "Easy like Sunday Morning," he was clearly *not* thinking about the effort it takes to get a family ready for an early morning church service. Those Sunday mornings are rarely easy and begin with bickering about who gets into the bathroom first, worries over what to wear, and desperate shouts: "Please, get in the car already! We're so late, we're going to be sitting in the front row!"

Despite all that, we make the effort, and almost magically those stressful moments along with countless other worrisome thoughts melt away as soon as we take a breath and join in the worship. For an hour (or longer depending on your particular brand of religion), there is peace, a feeling of unity with those around you, and the reminder that there is much more to this life than jobs, money, and *stuff*.

More than a third of Americans attend weekly worship services, according to 2015 Gallup polls. The reasons vary. Some people go to these services because they feel it's expected of them or because it's part of their family's heritage. Others find cathedrals, mosques, or synagogues to be uplifting places or places of refuge or solace. Many go seeking answers for their lives.

Americans are certainly not the only people who connect to others, themselves, and some form of higher power through faith practices. All cultures express faith and spirituality in some way. "Although the specific content of spiritual beliefs varies, all cultures have a concept of an ultimate, transcendent, sacred, and divine force,"[1] write Christopher Peterson and Martin Seligman in *Character Strengths and Virtues*. It seems that spirituality is an innate trait for humanity.

During the past several decades, researchers have linked greater life satisfaction with religious or spiritual practices. Differing from religion—which may include but isn't limited to attending worship services, being part of a church family, and identifying with an organized religion—spirituality runs deeper and is more personal or unique to the individual. A spiritual practice for one person may be sitting quietly in nature or doing yoga. For another, it may mean serving food to homeless people or practicing gratitude through prayer. Regardless of how faith is expressed, studies have repeatedly proven that spirituality—in any number of forms—enhances a person's life. The benefits include a having a sense of belonging and community, the feeling that you're not alone in the world; believing that your life is meaningful; and being equipped with the skills to cope with the stress and trials of life.

If you don't consider yourself a "religious" person, take heart. Although being part of a religious group can be extremely encouraging, we want to make it clear that getting in touch with one's soul—the essence of a person's being—does not require organized religion. Spirituality doesn't demand formal structures or rituals. Rather, it is the way we connect to ourselves, one another, and a higher power. It can be defined as *an inner belief system that you rely on for strength and comfort.*[2] That means a quiet hour in nature spent reconnecting with yourself can be as powerful as worshiping with a thousand other people during a service steeped in rich tradition. Both of these activities—along with countless other sacred moments—can feed the soul, nourishing and renewing it with hope and a sense of peace and belonging.

For the most part, people don't join a church or begin a spiritual practice with the intention of becoming happy. But it seems that when you come to a deeper understanding of who you are and how you fit into the grand design of life, happiness is what you find along the way.

We know that you, our readers, come from a variety of faith backgrounds and traditions. In the stories we share in this chapter, you'll see a few different ways that people draw on and express their spirituality. Even if your theology differs from those here, what we hope you'll take away from these inspiring accounts and the truths revealed at the end of this section is that faith is a very important part of your well-being.

Mathew Newburger

Finding Unconditional Love

Mathew Newburger has been an addict as long as he can remember. "It started with food when I was little. Then I smoked pot as a kid, and then it was drinking. The party never stopped." A back injury led to a dependency on opiates. "Eventually, I was a heroin addict," says the forty-three-year-old father of four. "Using was a constant in my life."

And so was God. Mathew was raised Catholic, and during one of his many brushes with the law as a teenager he was sent to a monastery to live with nuns for a few months. "I always had faith, but my guilt and remorse and shame for my addiction meant my belief in God made it worse," says Mathew. "God sees everything. How could he love me when I was a thieving heroin addict?"

By 2000, Mathew hovered near rock bottom. His addiction drove his construction business into the ground. Mathew fought bitterly with his wife, often throwing furniture, and he got into a fistfight with his brother. When his wife left and took the kids from their Colorado home to live near her mother in New Jersey, Mathew moved in with his own mother in Flushing, New York. He got construction jobs and was fired from them. He shoplifted anything he could find and resold the stuff—razors or chewing gum—to local bodegas for cash with which he bought drugs. "I'd get arrested and the cops would say, 'What are you doing with three hundred packs of gum?' I thought it was funny. They didn't think it was funny."

The First Step toward a New Life

Mathew considered suicide. "I knew that if I were dead, my kids would at least get Social Security," he says. "That overwhelming feeling of uselessness was my rock bottom."

Though he had attended Alcoholics Anonymous (AA) meetings off and on since he was fourteen, it wasn't until 2006, after yet another stint in rehab, that the recovery method and its spiritual teachings stuck. "I always thought I was smarter than everyone, that I was smarter than the program, that I could drink like a normal person," Mathew says. "I finally accepted that I am powerless over alcohol and drugs. That is when I got sober." In AA, the first two of the twelve steps to sobriety are admitting one's powerlessness over the addiction and recognizing that a "higher power," as defined by the addict, helps one get and stay clean. With his admission, Mathew had finally taken the first step.

Mathew still struggled with his understanding of a higher power. Then one day his sponsor sat Mathew down with a sheet of paper and a pen. The sponsor, who was himself an alcoholic who had worked through the twelve steps and was now helping Mathew navigate the journey to sobriety, instructed him to list all the negative things about his God that he struggled with. Mathew scribbled "guilt," "shame," and "anger." Then the sponsor drew a line down the middle of the paper and instructed Mathew to write in the second column the positive things about his God. He wrote "love," "compassion," and "unconditional acceptance."

"He ripped the paper in half, crumpled up the bad part, and tossed it aside. He said, 'Here's your God,'" remembers Mathew. "It was so simple, but it sticks with me to this day." That gesture forever changed Mathew's life. "I realized that God loves me no matter what. . . . God takes both the good and the bad in me, accepts me."

During his seven years of sobriety, Mathew's life has done a 180-degree change for the better. Today, three of his children live with him, as does his son-in-law.

Mathew's passion is stand-up comedy, and he has performed and hosted events at venues around New York City since becoming sober. "The more honest things are, the funnier they are," he says. "In my act, I share things about my past that I worry will embarrass my kids. But they tell me they are proud of me no matter what I've done."

This unconditional love has been a theme throughout his life since coming to a new understanding of God's love and willingness to offer second chances. Mathew's ability to accept and forgive himself—just as he believes God does—gives him the ability to attract that kind of love into many facets of his life.

Today, Mathew supports his family with construction work and is in a committed relationship. "My girlfriend knows everything about me. There are no secrets," he says. "In the past, all my relationships were so volatile—yelling, screaming, throwing things. In the past year, my girlfriend and I have not raised our voices once. For the first time I can be loving, compassionate, and tender toward another person in a way that I couldn't before. If I can act like that, that is God's way, I think."

Mathew fills his time with woodworking projects, creating custom furniture that he gives or sells to friends. He spends Sunday morning feeding homeless men at church-based shelters. But his favorite activity is spending time with his kids, talking with his three older daughters, and "acting like an immature boy and laughing" with his son. "My life is totally different today," he says. "I am not angry anymore. I don't lash out. I have a great relationship with my kids. I'm so grateful every day."

HAPPY ACT
Ask for Help

Admitting that you need help is often one of the first steps toward overcoming challenges. Ask a friend or spiritual leader for advice, or say a prayer for help.

Laura Benanti

Wishing Others Well

Imagine finding personal happiness without looking for it. Although it sounds unconventional, setting aside the desire to find her own happiness is exactly what put actor Laura Benanti on the path to spirituality, peace, and a deeper sense of contentment than she ever thought possible. "We all seek happiness for ourselves," says Laura. "And that seems like a natural thing to do, until you realize how that can actually impact your outlook."

"Self-cherishing, or focusing on your own happiness, sounds like it should be a wonderful thing," Laura continues. "And it may be to some extent, but by traveling my spiritual path, which includes meditation, I've found that, for me, self-cherishing leads to *unhappiness.*"

For years, Laura found herself on a road that many travel. She sought the comfort of good friends while she went through a painful divorce and focused on building a successful career. But looking for ways to boost her own happiness wasn't making Laura happy. And although she thought she was doing all the right things, something was missing. Then at age thirty-two, Laura changed her way of thinking.

Drawn to Buddhism at thirteen, Laura had been reading about and studying it ever since. "It was the spiritual path that made the most sense to me," she explains. But it wasn't until she was thirty-two and began meditating that Laura truly understood the role her spirituality played in her happiness. By regularly practicing mindful meditation, Laura learned to prioritize the happiness of others above her own. Scientists note that Laura's others-focused response to meditation isn't uncommon. Daily meditation, over time, changes physical connections in your brain so that, rather than having a me-focused thought or reaction to a negative circumstance, your automatic response is, first, the understanding that life isn't all about you and, second, a feeling of empathy toward others.[3]

Focusing on others' happiness opened her up to a unique sort of joy she never dreamed existed. "I think it's natural for us to look at happiness from our own perspective. So if a person cuts you off on the road, you think about how unhappy that makes you in the moment. If your heart is broken you look to be around people who can help put it back together and restore some sort of happiness." But now Laura found that putting herself in someone else's shoes and then wishing happiness for that person was what made her feel truly content.

"If I'm having a bad day, I can try to make myself happy in various ways like surrounding myself with friends or pouring a glass of wine. Or I can meditate on gratitude and how everyone who comes into my life creates an opportunity to practice empathy, kindness, patience, and love. Ultimately I choose to meditate on wishing true happiness and kindness and freedom to all beings."

Now, instead of getting angry or frustrated if someone cuts her off in traffic, she doesn't shout, swear, or get rattled behind the wheel. "I wish that person happiness. I don't know what's going on in their life and how those circumstances may influence their actions. They may be facing great struggles or hardship, so instead of thinking a fellow driver is a jerk, I hope the rest of his day is easier than his morning commute appears to be. Or that he reaches his destination safely and is happy once there."

Loving and Living Lighter

Meditation has helped Laura discover that wishing happiness for someone with her heart—not just with her head—without considering how that affects her own life lifts her spirits. "It feels good to want someone else to have a good day or experience. I feel much lighter doing that than getting upset and angry or thinking about how situations affect me." And although it's easy to wish happiness for someone she cares for, Laura's spiritual journey helped her realize that wishing happiness and peace for someone she's *not* emotionally attached to is especially good for her outlook. "If someone has harmed you or wronged you or said something to bruise your ego, and you're able to truly get yourself to a quiet space of wishing that person happiness . . . it's the most freeing feeling imaginable. I've found I can achieve tremendous happiness not by looking for it for myself, but by wanting it for others."

Her mind-set isn't one that always comes naturally. "I'm human, and my default is to want to prioritize my own happiness as being the most important thing." But practicing meditation daily has helped Laura boost her emotional well-being. "It's freeing to not be mired down by and consumed with your own happiness." That freedom has allowed Laura to clear a lot of stress from her life. It's also allowed her the emotional space to see happiness around her in unsuspecting places.

Laura is an actor, and rejection is a big part of her job. But wishing good things for those judging her performance as well as the competitors vying for the same roles has helped Laura enjoy every aspect of her job and focus on delivering her best performance rather than on outside distractions. "Actors hear, 'You're too tall, too short, too pretty, not pretty enough,' and so on. And I no longer take those comments personally, because I try to see the experience as a chance to learn something and wish those around me happiness. And doing so brings me joy even if I don't get the part."

Her spiritual practice has also taught Laura to slow down and helped her develop a sense of patience she didn't possess before. "I can be pretty impatient, but because of meditating and my approach to happiness, I'm kinder and more loving and less prone to anger. That can have such positive benefits for personal relationships.

"Being less concerned about every single moment of the day's being perfect for me and focusing on hoping the day goes well for others eliminate many sources of stress," she adds. For example, she no longer worries about what people say about her on social media. "I truly hope the person saying something negative or unkind has a nice day filled with love and kindness, because that's what they deserve. That's what we all deserve."

HAPPY ACT
Send Good Thoughts

The next time you're tempted to get angry or frustrated, stop, take a deep breath, and silently wish the other person a good day.

Stephanie von Hirschberg

Nature as Her Cathedral

New York City is a catalyst in many people's lives, but it made writer and editor Stephanie von Hirschberg "crave green." Once a regular church-goer, Stephanie had become "an experimenter," reading about different religions and soaking up knowledge about different forms of spirituality. And when she moved to the Westchester suburbs, she had an epiphany. Now, she says, "I know that what I'm saying is a cliché, but nature truly is my cathedral."

Stephanie is quick to say she doesn't "worship nature." Instead, she explains, "It's really more that there is some loving, healing energy that I sense, and it's something that is simple and uncomplicated. After I left Manhattan, I moved into a house that had a little garden. And I grew petunias on the porch—and those flowers, I would stare at them in amazement. I felt—I can only call it love—emanating from those pink petunias. It may sound a little corny, I am sure, but that is what I experienced."

"Now," she says, "it is not just what I see. It's what I hear—the bird-songs. There's a pond near my house, and the bullfrogs croak all through the night, and I just love that sound. I feel as if all the sounds, sights, and smells, all the hidden things that go on are all connected to something big, something much bigger than I am, something mysterious and very beautiful. The word 'numinous' . . . I love that word. That captures what nature is for me."

She now works at home, but Stephanie says, "I used to commute to New York City, an hour and a half every day. I would get home around seven thirty. I would feed my dog, put her in the car, and drive ten minutes to a park nearby, which at that point would be pretty much empty. And I would walk there—and it was like balm. An absolute balm. I would soak up all the green; it would completely clear my mind and I'd feel myself getting lighter and lighter."

Years after she gave in to her craving for green, Stephanie says the influences on her spirituality now come mostly "from Buddhism and mindfulness." She meditates, does yoga, and prays. "But I stopped looking for knowledge," she adds. "I don't look for *knowing* anymore. I sometimes tell my agnostic and atheist friends, 'If you've experienced kindness and love and generosity—and you know those qualities exist in the world— and then imagine all of that love and kindness and compassion bundled together in one big energy form, you could call that God.'"

Living in a State of Grace

When she prays, Stephanie says, "I pray to be open. I think what has evolved is my openness to the Divine. I can choose to be open. I guess that is what grace is. When you are in a state of grace, it's a startling awareness of love. I find that when I'm feeling anxious or angry, I can ask to open my heart. I can take some conscious steps to open myself to the love that is out there."

Stephanie incorporates meditation techniques into her spirituality practices, many of which rely on natural images, to calm herself down. If she's had a rough day or is dwelling on something that annoys her or makes her anxious, she replaces that thought with an image. "I will sometimes imagine a rose, a beautiful pink rose. And I will see that enormous rose in my mind's eye," she says. "And so I bring the rose into my mind. And it will dissolve whatever is there." Other times, she concentrates on her breathing and imagines herself "drawing nourishment up from the earth" through the soles of her feet.

Stephanie says, "It's important to get my mind out of the way. Sometimes I envision a huge space surrounding my thoughts, and that space is just empty. And that emptiness is a great source of joy and liberation. And the sky, and looking up at the stars at night is a sort of physical experience of that emptiness for me, this notion of vastness out there that is beyond comprehension."

As a child, Stephanie was a late bloomer. "I had great difficulty speaking, reading, and writing. Words didn't come to me very easily." Now she believes that the urge to put words to one's experience hinders a person from being in the moment, a state of being she describes as peaceful, beautiful, and joyful. "I think that being very close to the Divine, when you are in that presence, it's not verbal. It's really not verbal." In connecting to the earth, herself, and what she calls the Divine, Stephanie finds she needs no words at all to bloom.

HAPPY ACT
Go Outside

Go for a nature hike, dig in your garden,
or simply stroll through the park. Notice the feel
of the earth beneath your feet, the scent of the
plants you pass by, and the sounds of the birds
and animals around you.

Shane Claiborne

A Twist of Faith

Conversations with Shane Claiborne begin and end with laughter. Laughter when he talks about the pranks he and his buddies pulled, including rappelling down the side of a college dorm. Laughter when he recalls splashing through fire-hydrant waterfalls with neighborhood kids on a steamy summer afternoon. Laughter when he talks about the night he and a bunch of homeless moms and kids in Philadelphia outsmarted a fire chief who was caving to political pressure.

Turns out, the chief was trying to evict the women and kids from an abandoned church in North Philadelphia's "Badlands," an impoverished neighborhood known for drugs and violence, where they'd taken refuge from the cold autumn winds that swept off the Delaware River a few blocks away. The women had moved inside the church and were sleeping with their children on pews and on the floor in the unheated structure. Then the religious organization that owned the building wanted them out.

Shane and his buddies from Eastern University had visited the abandoned church to pray with the families and offer support. However, unbeknownst to the group, the city's fire chief had scheduled a surprise inspection for seven in the morning. The plan was to inspect the building, "discover" a bunch of fire code violations, and order everyone out; then the police would enforce the order.

But not all of the rank-and-file firefighters were on board. Later that night, two firefighters arrived to tip off the families and help bring the church up to code. By dawn, with Shane, his friends, the firefighters, and the mothers working all night, the church was in compliance with every requirement of the fire code: fire extinguishers, exit signs, wiring, everything. The chief arrived, stomped through the structure, and then left. The moms and kids stayed, and Shane Claiborne realized that he'd just stumbled into what he was supposed to do with his life.

The Simple Way

Shane Claiborne is a radical. Make no mistake about it. He emerged out of the Bible Belt of east Tennessee, spent some time in his youth as a self-professed Jesus freak, attended a prestigious Christian college, interned at arguably the largest, most affluent Protestant church in America, and did graduate work at Princeton Theological Seminary.

But Shane doesn't practice his faith in a traditional way. He does it by feeling his way along the path he senses God has laid out in front of him, one shaped by sleeping on the streets of Chicago with the homeless, working with Mother Teresa in Calcutta, and breaking bread with the oppressed, the tortured, and the abandoned. As he writes in his book *The Irresistible Revolution*, "I learned more about God from the tears of homeless mothers than any systematic theology ever taught me."

Pursuing this path has been Shane's single-minded purpose for two decades. It's not that he's left the traditional practices of religious life behind. Prayer, caring for others, scripture, contemplation, and Communion are the touchstones of his existence. No, it's more that he's returning to simpler, more spiritual roots.

He's left the big-mortgage church in favor of a small community church in his neighborhood. He lives in a fixer-upper row house in Philadelphia's "Badlands" neighborhood. Here, he's helped create a small, intentional community of six to eight men and women who pray and work together every day of their lives.

That community, calling itself "The Simple Way," is, as its website boldly declares, "a web of subversive friends conspiring to spread the vision of 'Loving God, Loving People, and Following Jesus' in our neighborhoods and in our world." It's a noble purpose. And fueled by their passion, the community members began getting the hang of how to do it. "When we started sixteen years ago, we were reacting to crises," Shane says. "We were feeding one hundred people a day and trying to help people with housing issues."

There are still crises, he says, but over the years his neighborhood has stabilized. Even when people have housing issues, they're likely to stay in the neighborhood. And now the community has aquaponic systems, gardens, rain barrels, and the ability to grow its own food. "One friend says we're trying to bring the Garden of Eden to North Philadelphia," he says.

But even the Bible's Garden of Eden had a touch of evil slithering around, and some days Shane and his friends help their neighbors simply by accompanying them through the dark times. For example, a young man was shot dead on his block. ("Gun violence is a big focus here," Shane says.) So the group supports its neighborhood by offering a loving presence and helping neighbors find ways to express their grief, their anger, and their expectation for a better day.

At one gathering, the neighborhood came together to follow the biblical injunction to "turn swords into plowshares." "We did a kind of welding workshop, got a forge, and heated some guns," he says. "Then the mothers who had lost kids to gun violence beat the guns into trowels." Using the trowels in the garden to grow food that would feed the next generation of kids was a powerful statement of the women's determination that love would triumph over hate, forgiveness over anger, good over evil.

Acts like these have only shined the light brighter on Shane and his personal brand of the Christian lifestyle—and are attracting attention from across the religious spectrum. Each year, he receives invitations to speak at more than a hundred events in a dozen or more countries and nearly every state. He has led seminars at Vanderbilt, Duke, Pepperdine, Wheaton College, Princeton, and Harvard. And he has been publicly recognized by religious superstars including Brian McLaren, one of *Time's* twenty-five most influential evangelicals in America; Archbishop Desmond Tutu; former president Jimmy Carter; and Tony Compolo, professor, pastor, author, and spiritual counselor to former president Bill Clinton.

If these guys are right, Shane may be onto something, with his simple, purposeful, and passionate approach to faith, and maybe, just maybe, we could learn something from him.

HAPPY ACT
Break Bread Together

Building community, even in large churches,
often begins over food. Start connecting by
inviting a few people to share a meal with you.

The Science Behind the Wisdom of Spirituality

Forgiven. Peaceful. Accepted. Purposeful. Connected. Thankful. Loved. These words run to the core of the human existence—they are how almost all humans long to feel. And, for many, spirituality provides the path to a deeper, more fulfilling life that includes each of these cherished emotions.

It's little wonder, then, that study after study has found a positive correlation between life satisfaction and spirituality. Many of these studies' facilitators try to explain faith in concrete terms with empirical evidence. For example, one study stated that "individuals with high levels of religious faith are associated with higher levels of life satisfaction, greater personal happiness, and fewer negative consequences of trauma."[4] Another study reported: "After gender, age, history of depression, and risk status were controlled, individuals who indicated that religion or spirituality was highly important to them were 73 percent less likely to be depressed."[5] And a study that involved participants from various religious backgrounds, including Christians, Muslims, Buddhists, Quakers, and Jews, found that "higher levels of spirituality (with or without religious involvement) were correlated with higher levels of self-actualization and life meaningfulness."[6] Still other studies connect practicing one's faith to longevity (up to seven additional years[7]) and better relationships.[8]

Of course, scientists (even those who consider themselves spiritual) aren't satisfied with chalking up these benefits to a supernatural source.

Science demands an explanation. *Why* do faith-filled people experience such incredible benefits? It turns out there are a few good reasons.

A Sense of Meaning

Faith can provide a context or framework that allows people to understand how they fit into the world.[9] Spirituality helps us make sense of our lives, the world, and our place in it—particularly when things aren't going well. For many, spirituality brings deeper meaning to life and, as we saw in an earlier chapter, cultivating meaning is one of the keys to a happy life. Christians, for example, may feel a sense of security reading Romans 8:38–39: "For I am convinced that neither death nor life, neither angels nor demons, neither the present nor the future, nor any powers, neither height nor depth, nor anything else in all creation, will be able to separate us from the love of God that is in Christ Jesus our Lord" (NIV). Similarly, those who practice Judaism may find a similar sense of belonging when they read Jeremiah 31:32: "I will place My law in their midst and I will inscribe it upon their hearts, and I will be their God and they shall be My people" (Torah).

Even if the higher power is an undefined being or source, for example the "universe" or "nature," a felt connection to that source as well as the belief that each person's life has value provides a sense of meaning.

A Social Network That Provides Community

It's possible to experience community through a variety of activities—volunteering, joining the Junior League, the Red Hat Society, a country club, or a church. Being part of *any* community in which people care about and look out for one another can add to your well-being, but shared beliefs can deepen relationships within a religious context. There's comfort in knowing you aren't alone.

Think of the summer potlucks, celebrations of weddings and new babies, food when you're sick, and help feeding loved ones after a funeral—there's a reason food, faith, and community naturally go together.

Continual Gratitude

We've already talked about the importance of gratitude, and it's a practice central to almost every religion. A grateful heart is a happy heart, and a study by the John Templeton Foundation found that faith seems to positively affect our gratitude. In one survey, 75 percent of the most religious respondents agreed with the statement, "I have so much in life to be thankful for," whereas only 39 percent of those considered nonreligious agreed.[10]

Lower-Risk Lifestyle

"Individuals make daily decisions that often involve how to treat others or how to assess lifestyle practices or health behaviors. Religious or spiritual involvement has been associated with greater gratefulness, forgiveness, altruism, less delinquency/crime, less substance abuse, better school performance, and more disease prevention activities," one study explains.[11] Because religious organizations typically encourage healthy, positive conduct, and discourage activities like substance abuse, promiscuous sexual behavior, and crimes that are known to increase premature mortality risks, churchgoers may have increased life-expectancy rates.

Prayer and Meditation Calm the Body, Mind, and Soul

Prayer, alone or with a group, provides an incredible sense of connection. The act acknowledges that we are just a small part of something much greater than ourselves. In those moments, when words of gratefulness, cries for help, or expressions of awe are spoken, the heart opens and we are able to connect with something that is both invisible and as close as our breath.

Like meditation, prayer removes the clutter from our minds. In meditation, we focus on a single thought—beauty, wholeness, love, compassion, God. In prayer, our thoughts turn toward God or another higher power. Prayers may focus on praise, worship, or gratitude or may be a way to verbalize one's own limitations and need for help. Prayer and meditation are simple ways to experience what psychologist and mindfulness teacher Elisha Goldstein refers to as *sacred moments*.

A sacred moment, Goldstein explains, inherently possesses spiritual qualities, such as gratefulness, a feeling of connection with and support from the transcendent, awe, or a deep sense of inner peace. Additionally, he says "They are imbued with descriptive qualities such as precious, dear, blessed, cherished, and/or holy." Goldstein's study focuses on how to experience more of these sacred moments—"day-to-day personal moments that are imbued with sacred qualities, which seem like time-outs from daily busy-ness, where a sense of stillness arises or occurs and where concerns of the everyday just seem to evaporate." These moments help us notice, appreciate, and experience life more fully.

He found that meditation, specifically mindfulness meditation, allows people to create sacred moments. "Eighty-nine percent of participants who were interviewed reported that the cultivation of sacred moments had led to a stronger awareness of what was sacred in life."[12]

Science measures, calculates, and reviews data for evidence. But when it comes to explaining the value of spirituality, surveys and tabulations fall woefully short. What's sacred or holy or spiritual can't fully be measured. To be understood, it must be felt with the heart.

get happy

Make time for a sacred moment. Take five minutes to simply be still and mindful of the goodness in your life.

Attend a religious service. Listen to the words of the songs and the message being shared by the speaker. Talk with the people around you and ask why they attend services at that particular church, synagogue, or mosque.

Appreciate nature. Go outside at night and look at the stars or take a walk on a nature trail. Get away from buildings and the noise of the city and experience the diverse beauty of nature.

Read a spiritual book. Inspirational messages can strengthen and encourage your spirit. Visit your local bookstore and browse the Religion/Spirituality section.

Pray. Try beginning and ending your day with prayer. If you've never prayed before, you can simply start by saying thank you for the blessings or good things in your life. If you're facing a challenge, pray for God's guidance or for courage or help.

GIVING BACK

Love and kindness are never wasted. They always make a difference. They bless the one who receives them, and they bless you, the giver.

—BARBARA DE ANGELIS

*T*hroughout this book, you've read about the many, often simple, practices of happiness—things you can do to live a happier life right now. And, yes, you *can* control how happy you feel at any given moment. What a beautiful truth! You have the ability to change your attitude, choose the way you respond to and interact with others, improve your well-being and relationships, and connect in meaningful ways with the world around you. If you've taken nothing else from this book, we hope you've come to believe that regardless of your circumstances, a happier life is within reach.

In all honesty though, as much as we want you to experience a deeply satisfying life, we have an ulterior motive: we want you to change the world. You see, if each of us can live happier every day, we can also give back and share a little happiness with others every day. More than simply being sustainable, happiness is renewable—minute by minute, Happy Act by Happy Act. That's why the final happy practice we'll discuss is sharing happiness.

It isn't uncommon to hear about people, particularly celebrities, who "give back" by using their status or wealth to benefit people less fortunate than themselves. And certainly, giving back this way is commendable. In fact, one of the stories you'll read in this chapter is about supermodel Niki Taylor and her involvement with the Red Cross. But sharing wealth or using one's status to influence change is only one aspect of what it means to spread happiness. You don't need fame or fortune to make the world a better place; all it takes is a generous spirit and the willingness to take action when you see a need.

In the pages that follow, you'll meet people who have devoted their lives to making others happy. Through small, intentional acts of kindness as well as community and nationwide efforts, these everyday heroes show us how we can all make a difference—one life and one Happy Act at a time. As you read their inspiring stories, think about the people you encounter daily. What are their needs? How are they hurting? What Happy Act could you do to brighten a person's day or completely change a life?

With each act of kindness or generosity and with every smile you share, you'll discover a truth that happy people the world over know: when you give of yourself, you not only make others happy; you give yourself a boost of joy.

Michele Larsen and The Joy Team

Changing Lives by Sharing Messages of Joy

Just before Thanksgiving in 2009, Michele Larsen and her six-year-old daughter, Taryn, set out to spread some joy. They decorated seventy-five cards with hearts and flowers and on each included a short, handwritten message scrawled crookedly with bright crayons and markers: "You are special." "I am thankful for you." "You are terrific." "Be yourself." "Enjoy the world."

Michele hoped to drop some joy into the lives of the strangers in Portland, Oregon, and Vancouver, Washington, who found these notes scattered around those cities. Simply knowing they were brightening someone's day made her happy. "The feeling that comes from making a positive difference is this amazing, warm, heart-opening, expansive goodness," she says.

Spreading joy with her daughter felt so meaningful that day, Michele immediately knew she wanted to go bigger, "to spread joy, optimism, and inspiration to millions of people." Billboards would be better, she decided. And with that decision, the seed for the idea of The Joy Team, Michele's nonprofit organization, was planted.

"You Make a Difference"

Michele's mother has a background in accounting and helped her submit the required forms to the state of Washington and the IRS, a process that took about a year. During that time, Michele met with friends and family members. "I told them about this wild idea of putting positive messages on billboards just for the sake of spreading joy. They liked it, and all pitched in to make it happen," Michele says. "Once other people saw them and enjoyed them and wanted to be part of it, our circle of support grew." The Joy Team has since shared more than 180 positive messages on billboards across the United States and Canada.

It's impossible to know exactly how these positive messages affect the drivers who see them, but Michele trusts that the people who need the encouragement will see them. Every once in a while she gets confirmation of that fact. For example, when The Joy Team put up a billboard in Portland, Oregon, that read, "You make a difference," Michele had no idea how profound an impact that simple message would make on a woman who saw the sign every day as she took her son to school.

After receiving devastating news, the woman had been contemplating suicide. By the time she noticed the sign, she had even planned how she would take her own life. The first time she read the billboard, she skeptically wondered what The Joy Team was selling. A day or so later, she was dropping her son off at school again. This time, as she read the words once again—"You make a difference"—she thought, "Wouldn't it be nice if that message is for me?" Morning after morning she drove by and wished the message was meant for her, until one day she decided it was. Those four words, the affirmation that *she* made a difference, saved her life.

Through tears, Michele read the woman's thank-you note sent via private Facebook message: "I came to think of this billboard as my friend—the one friend who knew what I was going through. Sounds silly to say a billboard saved my life, but I have to tell you, it was the only encouraging word I was receiving at the time. One kind thought, day after day, truly does make a difference."

Michele says it was humbling to know how significantly The Joy

Team's efforts had touched someone's life. True to her joy-disseminating style, she immediately shared the happy news with everyone involved with The Joy Team. In her thank-you note to her team, she wrote: "We have made people smile and laugh. We have encouraged and inspired people to believe in their dreams. We have reminded them that they are loved and worthy of everything they can imagine. We have helped people out of depression. And this morning I learned we saved a life. We did this."

Bringing Joy Through Positive Messages

"I've learned that doing something for others with the intention of bringing them joy is a powerful gift for everyone involved," Michele says. By following her purpose to share joy, Michele has discovered a lot about happiness. "I know that being happy is a choice, and everyone can make that choice—everyone. I also know now that not everyone wants to make that choice, and that was a little surprising to me." She acknowledges that it isn't always easy, but she believes all can choose the most positive thought in every moment with some practice. And she hopes The Joy Team's billboards will help people make that choice.

The Joy Team has been sharing joy for six years now, and its initiatives grow every year. The team leads a national Chalk the Walks day on the third Tuesday in August, when they write positive messages with brightly colored chalk on sidewalks and encourage people to join in coast to coast. The Junior Joy Team, middle-school students who hold boardroom-style meetings (complete with lollipops) to dream up ways to share happiness, have delivered joy packs in their Portland and Vancouver communities and wrapped peanut-butter jars bound for food pantries with positive messages.

And Michele continues to dream big. She hopes to see a billboard with a positive message up in every city. "There are people who need to hear it. What we see and think affects us. Surround yourself with as many positive messages as you can," she says. "We are all connected, like leaves on one tree. Whatever we do to help others helps us all. If we lift up enough people, we all rise."

HAPPY ACT
Leave a Note

Leave a positive note where a stranger is
sure to find it, on the mirror in a public restroom,
for example.

Kenrick Wagner

The Gift of Giving

Tragedy often spurs transformation. This certainly proved true for Kenrick Wagner when his sister passed away suddenly. He was twenty at the time, and the deep and unexpected loss prompted him to wonder what he could do with his life that really mattered. "I knew I needed to find direction in my life and meaning and purpose for life itself," he says.

Kenrick had always considered himself lucky to have grown up in a strong, loving family. Still, in the poverty-stricken area of the Bronx he called home, attaining the "good life" seemed almost impossible. Even as a teen, he wanted to be challenged to grow, but his school didn't have the kinds of programs and mentoring that more fortunate neighborhoods did. And though positive mentorship was scarce in his neighborhood, examples of lives destroyed by drug and alcohol abuse were prevalent. From the struggle and addiction that surrounded him, Kenrick knew what kind of life he *didn't* want. He just wasn't sure how to get onto the path toward a life he *did* want.

Finding Purpose

Kenrick didn't have money or even much life experience to share at the time, but he knew how to be a friend, how to show empathy, and how to motivate and encourage others. He decided to use those skills to help others.

"At the time, I wanted to get way from the inner city and do something I had never really done," Kenrick says. So he applied to work at a summer camp in Brewster, New York, more than sixty miles from the Bronx. In those new surroundings and with a fresh perspective, Kenrick knew that he had discovered his destiny in youth development. That was sixteen years ago.

Kenrick has since invested his life in developing programs and initiatives aimed at making sure at-risk youth have opportunities to find *their* good life and learn to pass on hope and opportunity to younger generations. "I found purpose in life, and my purpose is about helping youth. I am showing kids that there is more to life than the city; there is more in life to appreciate, and there is more to learn when you expand your mind."

He currently runs an after-school program and summer day camp for the Educational Alliance on the Lower East Side of Manhattan, serves as a motivational speaker for at-risk kids across the country, and leads his own youth-development consulting group that trains camp counselors to be team builders and to effectively connect with youth.

Connection, he says, is the key to helping people discover their potential. "You have to have awareness and be attuned to your neighborhood, your young people. You definitely have to be culturally relevant, and you have to know what they are going through. You have to be curious and ask questions. When we meet students who are in tough situations, they are just looking for someone they can relate to. You have to take a step back from yourself to be able to connect."

Change a Life, Change a Generation

Devoting his life to giving, mentoring, and connecting with at-risk kids changed his trajectory and kept him and countless others from becoming tragic statistics. He feels immense joy and pride when he sees people he has mentored through the years investing *their* lives in youth development and perpetuating a cycle of good. He knows his work has kept kids out of trouble and changed future generations by replacing despair with potential and hope.

He has kept up with some of the kids he has mentored and watched their progress. Many who grew up in the same rough neighborhoods

Kenrick came from—Brooklyn, Bed Stuy, and the South Bronx—are now flourishing in their own roles in youth development. Some have become leaders, counselors, and even camp directors for Education Alliance's after-school programs and summer camps. To Kenrick, seeing those kids—who are now teens and young adults—grow to become positive influences in their communities is the ultimate reward.

"So to see that, within a span of fifteen years, is one of the most amazing things," he says, "because we all know their lives could have gone in a totally different direction. They have made a turn for the good, and the people they have affected are making turns for the good. . . . It's a never-ending, rewarding experience."

One perhaps unexpected benefit of his work is the constant reminder that there is more to life than himself, and for Kenrick that knowledge is very therapeutic. "Sometimes, when we get in the four corners of our room, we kind of get down on ourselves, like there is no one else going through these things, and it's damaging. People turn to drinking or drugs," he says. "When I walk into a camp or an after-school program, I am constantly reminded that there is a world outside of myself. And to me that is refreshing. It keeps giving me purpose and motivation to do the work I do."

Helping others and putting them in a situation to pay it forward gives Kenrick a sense of personal fulfillment. "It is a continuum of giving, kindness, random acts of goodness in which you immediately see the return. When you see the people whose lives you've affected in a positive way and get inspired to give to this continuum, it is the most basic and raw sense of goodness on earth."

HAPPY ACT
Listen

Today, just listen. Part of empathy is allowing the
other person to be heard and understood.

Niki Taylor

The Gift of Time

Two seconds is all it took to change international supermodel Niki Taylor's life forever. One second she was appearing on runways and magazine covers all over the world, and the next, bleeding to death and fighting for her life in an emergency room. In 2001, Niki was critically injured in a car accident that left her liver severed. She needed more than one hundred units of blood from multiple donors just to stay alive.

Thankfully the hospital she was rushed to happened to be an American Red Cross donor facility. Today, she lives to tell her story because of the American Red Cross and the people who rolled up their sleeves to give blood. "I feel like the accident should have been the greatest tragedy in my life, but it wasn't; it was a blessing," Niki says. "Now it's my mission to get the word out about blood donation, because that's why I am here."

For nearly a decade the supermodel has been lending her name, time, and energy to the effort to encourage people to donate blood. Every June 14, on World Blood Donor Day, she teams up with the American Red Cross and the Nexcare Bandages Give Campaign to raise awareness about the need to maintain supplies during the summer months when accidents are at their peak. High-school and college students make up 20 percent of blood donors, and when school is out for summer break, donations are generally sluggish.

According to the American Red Cross, someone in the United States needs blood every two seconds. "No one knows this better than Niki Taylor," says Kara Lusk Dudley, Public Affairs Manager with American Red Cross. "The goal of this program is to inspire people to donate and to raise awareness about the ongoing need."

Niki also points out that five million people require blood transfusions annually and more than forty-one thousand donations are needed each day just to meet the needs of patients undergoing surgeries and chemotherapy treatments and keep the supply fresh. Blood outside of the living body can be stored for only forty-two days and platelets for five. Thankfully, Niki says, "One donation can save up to three lives."

A few years ago, Niki had an opportunity to express her gratitude in person as the American Red Cross—which numbers, scans, and tracks all of their blood donations—reunited her with the very same donors who gave the blood that was used to save her life. She remembers feeling a deep sense of gratitude and thankfulness that day and sensing the compassion that people have for one another to give just a little part of themselves to help make a live-saving impact. "I feel blessed because I got a second chance at life, thanks to blood donors," she says.

Throughout her time with the American Red Cross, Niki has heard countless touching stories from people who have had an experience similar to her own. A particularly moving story is that of Brian Boyle, a motivational speaker and current national volunteer spokesperson for the American Red Cross, who lost 60 percent of his blood from a car accident in 2004. She says that since his recovery, Brian has given back every drop of blood he lost in his accident and now participates in triathlons.

She admits that before the accident, she really didn't think about blood donation, even though her parents are lifelong donors. Now she surrounds herself with a culture of giving and pays it forward. Her husband, stock-car racer Burney Lamar, gives platelets and her parents belong to the "gallon club" and give blood every three months. "I love being a part of it," she says. "It's just something that is my mission now, and I get the word out any way I can."

She feels that giving back, even if it is something small like a kind gesture or big like a pint of blood, is a key component to happiness. Raised by a very giving and caring family, she heeds her parents' teaching that by giving of yourself and taking care of people, the giver actually receives the greater benefit. It's a lesson that she has passed down to her own children. "It's good for the soul to look out for one another," she says.

In the moments after the accident and subsequent surgeries, she became even more aware of what a gift life truly is. She also makes sure to acknowledge all the good she has in her life.

Whether it is having that chance to have one more day with her family, listening to the sound of her purring cats, or running on a fresh spring day, Niki says it's being appreciative of every moment that creates a beautiful life. "There is a lesson in every moment and every moment is a gift," she says. It only takes two seconds to change someone's day, Niki says. "Every day you need to smile at people, say hi to one another, and give someone a compliment. You can turn someone's bad mood into a good one."

HAPPY ACT
Donate Blood

Find a center and make a blood donation. If you can't donate blood for some reason, volunteer to pass out juice and cookies at a local blood drive.

Monya Williams

Can Happy Acts Change Me?

In May 2014, Monya Williams lost her smile. For five years, she'd fought, prayed through, and survived stage III breast cancer, uterine cancer, and the removal of the mastoid bone from her right ear. She'd lost her breasts, her uterus, and the hearing on her right side. But nothing could have prepared her for the devastation she felt when her doctor told her she would never smile again.

Monya had become an expert at fending off the feelings of despair and depression that accompanied chemo, radiation, painful surgeries, and a medicine cabinet full of prescription drugs. More than once, unspeakable pain and weariness caused her to consider the upside of death. Her private journal and public blog provided a place to work through raw emotions, and her faith gave her the strength to cling to hope. Even so, some days felt unbearable; May 21, 2014, was one of those days.

Two weeks earlier, just a few days after the surgery to remove the mastoid bone from her right ear, excruciating pain woke Monya in the middle of the night. The relentless, searing ache couldn't be numbed, even with the prescribed post-op painkillers. When she looked in the mirror later the next morning, she didn't recognize her reflection. The entire right side of her face sagged. She tried to return her lips to their normal position, but they wouldn't budge. Nor could she open her right eye. With a follow-up appointment already scheduled at Phoenix's Mayo

Clinic for noon that day, she headed in a little early. The doctor immediately admitted her to the hospital and began running tests.

At first, Monya and her doctors thought the facial paralysis was a temporary side effect caused by the surgery. But on May 21, the doctor explained to Monya and her husband, Eric, that her face would never return to "normal." A nerve in her face had died as a result of an infection following the surgery. Monya remembers trying to listen as the doctor, whose voice suddenly sounded to her like Charlie Brown's teacher, presented a few options to help improve the strokelike disfigurement, but all she really heard was that no amount of surgery or physical therapy would bring back her smile.

A New Outlook

Monya spent the rest of the afternoon at the Mayo Clinic going through follow-up procedures. Numb from the news she'd just received, she quietly watched people go in and out of the doctor's office while she waited for her name to be called. "Some were bald, some carried chemo packs in backpacks. I was trying every way I could to have a pity party; then someone else would step off the elevator and give me a new perspective: a man with one leg being pushed in a wheelchair by a not so patient wife, so many people wearing oxygen tanks."

Noticing people and acknowledging their needs wasn't new for Monya. Earlier that year, inspired by the International Day of Happiness, she had set a personal goal to do at least one "Happy Act"—an act of kindness, compassion, gratitude, or generosity—every day. Since then, she'd become intentional about looking for people who needed her help. And on that day in May, one of the most difficult of her life, her newly formed habit of simply acknowledging that people everywhere were suffering and in desperate need of happiness served her well. Noticing others' pain didn't erase her own or keep her from questioning, "Why me?" but it helped her remember that she wasn't alone—there were always people who needed her help. That's when she began to understand how her habit of helping others had helped her.

When Monya set her goal of 365 days of Happy Acts on the International Day of Happiness earlier that year, she had an ulterior motive: happiness was what *she* needed. She had seen a few presentations from happiness experts that day and heard one that explained how acts of kindness could bring joy—to both the recipient and the giver. The talk inspired her to join *Live Happy*'s #HappyAct movement. After what felt like a lifetime of pain and successive surgeries, she knew something had to change if she was going to be happy—so why not her? "My hope for doing these acts was purely selfish. I honestly wanted to see if my life would change if I was able to accomplish this incredible goal," she says.

When Monya set her goal, she wasn't certain she could reach it because of upcoming surgeries, including the one that would eventually rob her of her smile. So she kept her intention to herself and kept track of her progress by marking hearts on her planner to note the Happy Acts she did each day. She'd hoped the Happy Acts would make her happier, but, until she lost her smile, she didn't just realize how significantly the simple practice of noticing and helping others had changed her outlook on life.

Intentional Acts of Happiness

To have any hope of accomplishing her goal, Monya knew she would have to be intentional about it, but she wanted situations to unfold naturally; she didn't want to plan whom she was going to help. Her goal was to become aware of people's needs and to be ready to respond in an appropriate way. "Most of my daily acts of kindness were given without any extra time or money out of my pocket. Just opening a door for someone or helping a mother struggling with her children in the grocery store," she says.

Sometimes, she'd take a box of cookies to a school and give them to the staff in the administration office. She kept small bills on hand to give to people in need. She helped people to their cars at the Mayo Clinic, bought lunches and dinners for random people, took snack boxes to chemo and radiation units at different facilities monthly, and wrote notes to let people know they were loved and appreciated. The size and cost of the act didn't matter; the message of compassion, showing other people that someone cared for them, is what counted. And every act of kindness rewarded *her* with happiness.

Today, she can flip through her daily planner full of hearts and count the lives she's touched—and be reminded of how those people touched her life in return. For some of those experiences and people, however, she needs no reminder—they are etched in her memory. John is one of those people. She first met him when he was living under a bridge near her workplace. Twice a week she took him a loaf of bread, peanut butter and jelly, potato chips, and cookies or cupcakes. "I also made him a blanket for the winter months," she says. John had become part of her happiness routine, so when he disappeared from his spot under the bridge, she worried about his safety.

Months went by without any sign of him. Then one day, she recalls, "I was shopping at Wal-Mart when a man walked up to me with tears in his eyes. I didn't recognize him and it frightened me." The man was clean-shaven, his hair was neatly styled, and he wore a Wal-Mart vest. Slowly, it dawned on her that this was John from under the bridge. With tears running down his cheeks, he said, "Ma'am, I will forever be grateful to you for showing me kindness; no one has ever been so kind to me. It gave me strength to get up, find some local help, and get a job. You changed my life."

Monya says, "I was so overwhelmed with love in that moment, I couldn't help but grab him and hug him tight. He had no idea what he did for me, and I will never be able to repay him for the lesson I learned from him." Kindness in small doses, like sandwich makings and a warm blanket, can profoundly impact the course of a person's life.

On March 20, 2015, Monya Williams celebrated 365 consecutive days of Happy Acts by planning an entire day of happiness. In conjunction with the International Day of Happiness, she set up Happiness Walls at two elementary schools in her area where children and staff wrote about how they would share happiness. She spent time playing with her grandsons. And one of the Happy Acts she planned that day was to surprise a stranger with a financial gift. After waiting and watching people at a gas station for more than an hour, she finally saw the woman she knew she needed to help. Monya walked up to the station attendant and paid for a full tank. Monya then handed the delightfully shocked woman $100.

One Happy Act after another filled the day, and Monya's life, with powerful, positive memories. "I can honestly say, I am a different person now than I was a year ago," Monya says. What started as a yearlong goal became a lifestyle. She can't imagine a day going by without engaging with others through kindness or compassion, for their benefit—and for hers. "Knowing there is always someone in the world who is worse off than I am has helped me to stay out of my pity party and concentrate on others." Though she would love to have her smile back, Monya says the joy she's experienced by being so focused on helping others has enabled her to cope with her own suffering. "It has really saved me and helped me to get out of a deep, dark place that I had been in for a really long time; acts of compassion brought happiness and brightness back into my life."

Acknowledging others' suffering helped her remember that as dark and painful as cancer had made her life, she could still choose to bring joy to people's lives. And maybe that's the real lesson: happiness is a choice. When you choose to encourage others by showing compassion even in the smallest ways, their smile brightens your life in return.

HAPPY ACT
Make Small Gestures

Small acts of kindness can make a lasting impression.
Hold the door open for someone today!

Stacy Kaiser

Helping, Her Way

"I was raised to believe that you always give back," says Stacy Kaiser, a Los Angeles–based psychotherapist, media personality, and author. She and her brother grew up stuffing envelopes for charity and helping their parents collect food for the homeless. Those experiences fostered within her a heart for the hurting—the desire to "help people in crisis who didn't have the money to get help." So after completing her master's degree in psychology, Stacy joined a nonprofit that served people facing dire circumstances. "The place where I was working helped *so* many people—small children, pregnant teens, victims of abuse, and people who had horrible traumas."

Then, after ten years of working full time with the nonprofit, Stacy's own life turned upside down. "I unexpectedly found myself the single parent of my two daughters," she says. "I always thought I'd be raising kids with a partner, and so to suddenly be by myself was shocking and confusing." Thankfully, her experience helping others had equipped her with valuable coping skills, as well as the support she needed to create her new normal. "I had friends who do what I do, so I got lots of advice and support for free. I was lucky I had access to the resources that I had."

Her awareness of that luck stayed top of mind when she made the transition to private practice. Her family's financial well-being had dictated the switch, but she still wanted part of her life to be about giving back. And now she was particularly sensitive to the needs of solo parents.

"Back then, I used to wish I could give something away for free to let people know how much I cared," Stacy says. "I used to think that if I owned a restaurant I could give away free meals. If I was a hairdresser I would give out free salon services. One day it hit me—I *did* have something to give away. I could offer support, advice, and tools to people so that they could live happier, more fulfilling lives—and I could do it for free! That realization, and taking action on it, has brought me great joy."

Soon, single parents who needed advice and support heard about Stacy's practice—and her willingness to help even those who couldn't afford therapy. In addition to her paying clients, Stacy offers help on a pro bono basis to about three clients at one time. One such client, a mom we'll call "Tammy," has been coming to Stacy (and insisting on paying whatever she can) for ten years. "Tammy is one of those naturally happy people. She lights up a room. But her light was being snuffed out by her circumstances." Her three children's dad was, says Stacy, "out of the picture."

Both women's children were under ten years old when they first met. Tammy was raised by a cold, controlling mother and absent father, so she had no good role models for how to parent well. "But she loves her kids, and she's kind and nurturing," says Stacy. "She wanted more for them than she'd had for herself." That meant that if one of her children wanted music lessons, Tammy went without new clothes. "I remember her wearing these old, tattered shoes," says Stacy. "She really sacrificed to make her children happy. She was highly motivated and determined to give her kids more than she had had."

Today, Stacy looks back with satisfaction at all she and Tammy have come through together—and in their own lives. "We kind of grew up together as single moms. Now, we both have kids applying to college. It's easy to connect with her because we've done it together."

For Stacy, there's a great sense of satisfaction that comes from seeing how her work and passion for helping others is affecting the next generation. Tammy's children are thriving, and all three have gotten college scholarships. "One is already out of college, and she's working to help the needy. I can't take credit, but it's nice to know I played a small part."

HAPPY ACT
Use Your Talents for Good

Undoubtedly, your unique personality traits and life experiences equip you to help others in some way. Maybe you are a great listener who could volunteer on a crisis hotline. Maybe you're a decent cook and could prepare an extra serving of dinner for an elderly neighbor. Or maybe you could put your computer skills to work by creating the bulletin for your community center or place of worship. What are your gifts or talents? Whatever they are, using them to serve others will bring a smile to your face.

The Science Behind the Wisdom of Giving Back

Monya Williams committed to doing a year's worth of Happy Acts because she wanted to see if doing so really could change her life, and it did. In fact, every one of the people we interviewed told us that giving to others—whether of their time, money, or influence—made them feel better, *happier.*

Renew Your Happy Reserves by Helping Others

Science offers an explanation for this feel-good phenomenon. Researchers call the rewarding feelings experienced after engaging in "prosocial behavior" a "helper's high." Performing intentional acts of kindness and generosity—even something as simple as smiling at a stranger—triggers the brain to release the same rush of endorphins felt when being the recipient of a gift.

The response your body has to sharing happiness is a measurable, physical reaction that proves happiness is renewable. A study from Stanford University and Harvard Business School cites research that indicates people who give even small amounts of time, energy, or money to help others often feel a profound sense of reward. For example, studies show that volunteer work has "been associated with higher levels of life satisfaction, greater happiness, and fewer symptoms of depression."[1]

So if your happy reserves are running low because you've received bad news or had a rough day, you can improve how you feel by helping someone.

It really is that simple! This helper's high is why Kenrick Wagner feels a rush of pride when he sees the young adults he's mentored reach out to others in their community. And it's why Monya Williams says that she would endure the pain of cancer again to experience the fulfillment she gets from helping others. The brain rewards us with happy feelings for doing good!

Giving Back Is Good for You

The body's chemical response to doing Happy Acts doesn't stop with a temporary emotional lift. Over time, the benefits of generous or kind behavior seem to compound. Researchers at Emory University found that giving help to others protects overall health twice as much as aspirin protects against heart disease.[2]

Those who volunteer one hundred hours a year, an average of just under two hours a week, receive the most substantial benefits. People fifty-five and older who volunteer for two or more organizations have an impressive 44 percent lower mortality rate in a five-year period—and that's after sifting out other contributing factors, including physical health, exercise, gender, harmful habits like smoking, and marital status.[3] The effect is stronger than exercising four times a week or going to church. This means that volunteering is nearly as beneficial to our health as quitting smoking!

The obvious question one could ask is: Aren't people who volunteer healthier in the first place? It's a valid question, but research shows that even people who suffer from chronic pain tend to report lower levels of pain after they begin volunteering.[4] Volunteering or giving of oneself in other ways creates a self-reinforcing cycle: people who do good feel good, and people who feel good do good.

Share Freely, Without Imposing Expectations

Science clearly shows that Happy Acts benefit the giver as much as, and sometimes even more than, the recipient. However, researchers warn that helping someone with the *expectation* that your actions can make that person happy—a broad and hard-to-measure outcome—can set you up for disappointment. It's better to set well-defined goals. Monya's focus, for example, was showing compassion to others. Her own life experiences had taught her that everyone deals with painful circumstances. "My pain is visible; everyone can see my face. But so many people walk around with pain—mental, emotional, physical—that we can't see," she says. So rather than focusing on making others happy, she set out with the intention of noticing people's needs and offering kindness or help without showing judgment regarding their circumstances. Her expectation was that *she* would be kind, not that someone would respond in a particular way.

Additionally, just as Michele Larsen experienced, Happy Acts don't need to be monumental to make a difference in someone's life. If you can afford to give away $100 to someone who has fallen on hard times, that's great. Go for it! But don't discount the benefits of small acts and non-financial gifts, like positive messages handwritten on homemade cards. Easily repeated gestures, such as using someone's name when showing sincere appreciation or lending a hand to a mom who is struggling to simultaneously keep up with her grocery cart and her child, can make a difference in that person's life. And the emotional rewards you'll experience may be even greater than those felt after giving a large, one-time gift.

Create a Kindness Ripple Effect

Kenrick wanted to help his community by reaching out to at-risk youth. His goal wasn't to change one life, but many by encouraging kids to "pay it forward." Likewise, Niki Taylor helps the American Red Cross keep its blood banks full by encouraging others to donate blood. And they have, just as the kids Kenrick has worked with have gone on to help others. The reason both Niki and Kenrick are getting the results they desire is because kindness creates a ripple effect. In other words, Happy Acts are contagious.

"Upstream reciprocity" is a term researchers use to describe the response humans have to experiencing—or even just seeing or hearing about—the kind or generous behavior of others. A 2010 study by researchers James Fowler and Nicholas A. Christakis found that for every act of kindness a person received, he or she would naturally reciprocate (without being asked or prompted) by helping three other people.[5] Imagine what your family and community could look like if every person shared happiness with three other people. Ripples could turn into waves!

Can giving back make a real difference? Michele Larsen, Kenrick Wagner, Niki Taylor, Monya Williams, and Stacy Kaiser certainly believe so. They each live happier every day, because they've chosen to intentionally seek out people who need kindness, guidance, or a simple smile. The impact of giving back, though at times hard to measure, can't be discounted. If positive words on a billboard can save a person's life, there's no doubt that your generosity could brighten someone's day. Because here's the truth: *you* make a difference.

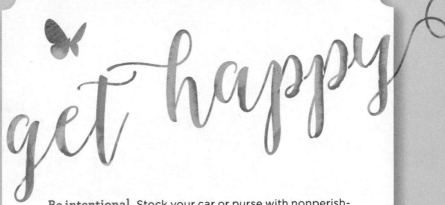

Be intentional. Stock your car or purse with nonperishable foods to give away to people in need.

Be aware. Watch for people who might need your help.

Be compassionate. Simple acts of kindness can take people by surprise and brighten their day—and yours!

Be realistic. Don't expect to make someone else happy. Smaller goals (e.g., eliciting a smile) are easier to reach and therefore tend to be rewarding to the receiver and the giver.

CLOSING HAPPY THOUGHTS

Chances are, you've read this book because you want to be happier. You're probably not *un*happy. You're optimistic and purposeful enough to have bought and read this book. Still, you want to be *happier.*

You're not alone. We all want to feel less stressed, more peaceful, and more connected to the people we cherish. And we're *all* works in progress.

That's right, even the folks who research and write about happiness all day long don't have it all figured out. *Live Happy* headquarters isn't Olympus, where perfect, godlike employees dictate how people can and should add joy and meaning to life. We're just like you—an imperfect bunch of women and men who were drawn to this work because we are interested in becoming happier ourselves. Luckily for us—blessedly for us—we derive great meaning from what we do, and this in itself makes us happier. But, again, we're works in progress, just like you. And we hope that you, like us, have been inspired, enlightened, and encouraged by what you've read in this book.

You may have seen yourself in Tory Johnson, who needed to make what she called her "shift"—a significant, life-changing decision that she was finally going to do something about being overweight. Or perhaps the story of Holly and Ben Raynes stuck with you because you too are going about your life's routine with a hunk of your soul missing—and you need to express your creativity to feel truly alive again. Or maybe life has dealt you a very difficult card, like "Joannie from Pringle," who was told she had pancreatic cancer and only a short time to live, or Kristen Meekhof, who lost her husband very suddenly at age thirty-three, and the shift you want or need to make is about going on and making the best of life.

We hope the stories and wisdom we've shared in these pages have allowed you to take a big step forward in your happiness journey. But although big steps are often important and necessary, we don't want you to miss the trees for the forest, because even if you need to take a giant leap, living a happy, vibrant, meaningful life isn't ultimately about the big stuff. Sure, a decision, like Kerry Stallo's, to leave a joyless job for a whole new career is a very big deal. But she got there step by step. She had to get training and certifications. She had to figure out how to live on much less money. In other words, she had to make day-by-day, moment-to-moment decisions to live happy. And so do we all.

In this journey toward a happier life, each of us must ask ourselves: What can I do to live happier *today*? How can I share a little joy *today*?

Those two questions reveal the heart of this book, because happiness isn't about if-onlys or perfect timing, but about what you can do, right now, in this moment, to experience and share happiness. Living a truly happy life isn't about grand gestures or extravagant displays of love or generosity. Sure, those are nice. But often a note posted on the bathroom mirror can mean just as much as an expensive gift, because though the thought counts, the *act* that follows the thought is what brings a smile to someone's face—and to your own.

We learned from the director of *Pursuing Happiness,* Adam Shell, that the expression is the experience. In other words, what we put out into the world is what we experience right now—not later, when and if that good feeling or act of kindness makes its way back to us—but right here and now in the moment. Moment to moment, that's how we experience happiness. So we better stop waiting for the if-onlys.

In discussing the happiness practice of taking care of our health, Tory Johnson said that if someone had told her it would take a year to lose sixty-two pounds and that she would have to make significant changes in her life to do it, she would have said no. A year would have simply felt too long, like an eternity. But a year passed in a blink, and a million tiny choices added up to a healthier body and an even happier life. The same principle applies to each one of the happiness practices. Tiny choices—attitude shifts, the choice to be grateful rather than complain, the decision to keep living when tragedy strikes, an act of kindness—these thoughts and actions and countless others add up to create a life that is at once full and completely expended, rich, joy-filled, and happy.

Positive psychology—which truly began when Martin Seligman inspired his psychology research colleagues to invest their energy in studying how to help the average person thrive, rather than focusing solely on mental disorders—is a mere two decades old. Science has since made great strides in understanding the *how* of happiness, but we still have much to learn. One thing we know with certainty is that the potential to live happier exists within each of us.

At *Live Happy* we will continue to share uplifting stories, resources, and the latest research, because we know that when you find joy in your life, you can in turn help others *live happy*.

Before You Go . . .

We invite you to share your happiness stories with us! We would love to hear which Happy Acts from this book you've tried and whose story resonated with you and why. Hearing from our readers makes us happy, so share the love and send us a note at editor@livehappy.com. Or join the Happiness Movement at LiveHappy.com. And if you just made someone smile, post a note on social media and tag it #HappyActs.

Here's to your very happy life.

ACKNOWLEDGMENTS

I feel blessed that my work reminds me daily of the importance gratitude plays in happiness, and I have so many people to be grateful for in my life. A ton of work and inspiration went into the creation of this book, and there is no way that I can fully express my appreciation to everyone involved, but I am willing to try!

First, a special thanks to Jeff Olson. His dedication to making people better led to the founding of the magazine and eventually to the crafting of this book. I hope we continue to make the world a better place through Live Happy for years to come.

Also, I cannot thank the people who shared (and continue to share) their stories with us enough. They provide inspiration to me every day.

Many people contributed to the creation of this book, but it would not exist without the tireless writing and editing skills of Erin K. Casey. Her ability to deliver quality work under very short timelines is second to none. Thanks also to Susan Kane for her editing prowess and story wrangling. She rolled up her sleeves to gather many of the stories in this book that bring tears to my eyes. Paula Felps, *Live Happy*'s science editor, simply blows me away with all of her insight, knowledge, and diligence. I want to thank her for putting so much of herself into this book and into *Live Happy* magazine. Kathryn Finney, Live Happy's creative director, is responsible for the great look of *Live Happy* magazine, and art-directed the fabulous chapter illustrations in this book. I could not ask for a better eye or a more dedicated person when it comes to creating the Live Happy brand. Also a special thanks to Donna Stokes, *Live Happy*'s managing editor, both for her wonderful story ideas and for keeping the magazine going no matter the craziness around us.

I must thank the wonderful team at HarperCollins and HarperElixir, including our publisher, Claudia Boutote, who made this book happen; our terrific senior editor, Libby Edelson, who made it better; and our production editor, Lisa Zuniga, who made it right. Also, thank you to our agent, Heidi Krupp, who had the vision before I did, and the K2: Krupp Kommunications team for believing in Live Happy. It is a joy to work with a team that brings so much professionalism and dedication to their work.

Through their contributions of writing, research, and ideas for this book, *Live Happy* magazine editors Chris Libby, Shelley Levitt, and Emily Miller are all deserving of my thanks. Dozens of people—writers, editors, artists, designers, photographers, and more—play a part in putting *Live Happy* magazine together each month, and I can't say thank you enough to all of them. For this book, we reached out to staff members as well as many of our regular contributors, and I would like to recognize the following for their specific contributions:

Melissa Balmain—*Celeste Peterson: Always a Mom*

Sandra Bienkowski—*Michele Larsen and The Joy Team: Changing Lives by Sharing Messages of Joy*

Timothy Bloom—*Arianna Huffington: Everything Can Wait* and *Shawn Achor and Michelle Gielan: When Happiness Experts Fall in Love*

Erin K. Casey—*Monya Williams: Can Happy Acts Change Me?; Tory Johnson: A Shift for Good; Gary and Vicki Flenniken: More to Love; Dan Miller: Helping Others Succeed;* and *Adam Shell: Pursuing Happiness.*

Katya Cengel—*Sabriye Tenberken: The Beauty of Blindness*

Christina Boyle Cush—*Rebecca Weiss: Delivering Cheer* and *Billi Kid: Reinventing Himself*

Sally Deneen—*Joan Lewis: The Power of Gratitude*

Stephanie Dolgoff—*Writing Myself Happy*

Paula Felps—*Mary Miller: Discovering and Achieving Dreams* and *Rhonda Cornum: Soldiering On*

Annie Bergman Giattina—*Ryan Bell: Giving with a Thankful Heart*

Emma Johnson—*Judy Kirkwood and Gretchen Brant: Friends for Life's Ups and Downs; Lauren and Mark Greutman: Thriving After a Financial Crisis;* and *Mathew Newburger: Finding Unconditional Love*

Chris Libby—*Kenrick Wagner: The Joy of Giving* and *Niki Taylor: The Gift of Time*

Jamie Malanowski—*Jason Mraz: Say Yes to Life* and *Levon Helm: Finding a New Voice*

Kristin A. Meekhof—*The Healing Power of Gratitude*

Ellen Michaud—*Shane Claiborne: A Twist of Faith*

Megan Michelson—*Natalie Wilgoren: One Step at a Time*

Lisa Ocker—*Kerry Stallo: Jumping Off the Career Track* and *Gretchen Rubin: Savoring the Moment*

Patty Onderko—*Ben and Holly Raynes: Making Creativity a Priority*

Robert Piper—*Alanis Morissette: Ever Mindful*

Gina Roberts-Gray—*Hoda Kotb: Looking Forward* and *Laura Benanti: Wishing Others Well*

Matthew Robinson—*Alastair Moock: Performing a Service*

Linda Rodgers—*Stephanie von Hirschberg: Nature as Her Cathedral*

Marie Speed—*Jenn Lim and Tony Hsieh: Happy at Work* and *Barb Schmidt: On Becoming Mindful*

Stephanie Wood—*Susan Bender Phelps: Taking Note of the Good; Brandon Mancine: Committed to Gratitude;* and *Roy Rowan: Ninety-Five Years Young*

Thank you to the entire staff at Live Happy for your dedication to making this world a happier place, and especially to Laura Coppedge, Chance Spann, and Joseph Panetta, who have been here from the start. What we are building together brings me great joy. I hope each one of you sees the blessing we have been given to have such meaningful work.

I would also like to thank Stuart Johnson, without whom Live Happy would not exist and I would likely be doing something far less interesting and fulfilling.

It is a wonderful thing to get to work in the happiness space. Nearly everyone we have asked has agreed to be interviewed or to write something for us. The overwhelming sentiment in this space is one of people supporting what we are trying to do. I can't name everyone but it would be remiss not to thank Shawn Achor and Michelle Geilan and their team at Good Think; Senia Maymin and Margaret Greenberg, Gretchen Rubin, Dr. Martin Seligman, and the many, many people who perform research into positive psychology; the people at the VIA Institute on Character, including Neil Mayerson and Ryan Niemiec; filmmakers Adam Shell and Nicolas Kraft; Stacy Kaiser; and the many, many others who have shared content and ideas with us.

The journey that led me to Live Happy started in my childhood home with my parents, Jim and Inge Heisz, who instilled in me a respect for others, a strong faith in God, and a few great values, not the least of which are honesty and perseverance. But the most valuable lesson I learned from them is that we only have so much time on earth, and we should use it to do the things we love with the people we love. I am fortunate to get to spend most of my days doing just that. And last, thank you to my family—Katie, Zach, Emma, and Quinn—for your unending and unqualified love and support. You are my purpose and meaning.

NOTES

Introduction

1. Sonja Lyubomirsky, Kennon M. Sheldon, and David Schkade, "Pursuing Happiness: The Architecture of Sustainable Change," *Review of General Psychology* 9(2) (2005): 111–31.

The Truth About Happiness

1. Martin Seligman, *Flourish: A Visionary New Understanding of Happiness and Well-being* (New York: Free Press, 2011).

2. Ed Diener and Martin Seligman, "Very Happy People," *Psychological Science* 13(1) (January 2002): 81–84.

3. Barbara L. Fredrickson, "The Value of Positive Emotions," *American Scientist* 91 (July–August 2003): 330–35, http://www.unc.edu/peplab/publications/Fredrickson_AmSci_English_2003.pdf.

4. Ed Diener and Robert Biswas-Diener, *Happiness: Unlocking the Mysteries of Psychological Wealth* (Malden, MA: Wiley-Blackwell, 2008).

5. Laura D. Kubzansky and Rebecca C. Thurston, "Emotional Vitality and Incident Coronary Heart Disease: Benefits of Healthy Psychological Functioning," *Archives of General Psychiatry* 64(12) (December 2007): 1393–401.

6. Laura D. Kubzansky, Laurie T. Martin, and Stephen L. Buka, "Early Manifestations of Personality and Adult Health: A Life Course Perspective," *Health Psychology* 28(3) (May 2009): 364–72.

7. D. A. Snowdon et al., "Linguistic Ability in Early Life and Cognitive Function and Alzheimer's Disease in Late Life: Findings from the Nun Study," *Journal of the American Medical Association* 275(7) (February 21, 1996): 528–32.

8. Maruta, Toshihiko et al., "Optimists vs Pessimists: Survival Rate Among Medical Patients Over a 30-Year Period," *Mayo Clinic Proceedings* 75(2): 140–43.

9. Susan David, Ilona Boniwell, and Amanda Conley Ayers, eds., *Oxford Handbook of Happiness* (Oxford: Oxford Univ. Press, 2013), 126.

Attitude

1. Barbara L. Fredrickson, *Love 2.0: Finding Happiness and Health in Moments of Connection* (New York: Hudson Street, 2013).

2. M. F. Scheier and C. S. Carver, "Effects of Optimism on Psychological and Physical Well-being: Theoretical Overview and Empirical Update," *Cognitive Therapy and Research* 16(2) (April 1992): 201–28.

3. M. V. Mondloch, D. C. Cole, and J. W. Frank, "Does How You Do Depend on How You Think You'll Do? A Systematic Review of the Evidence for a Relation Between Patients' Recovery Expectations and Health Outcomes," *Canadian Medical Association Journal* 165(2) (July 2001): 174–79.

4. Michael Mendelsohn, "Positive Psychology: The Science of Happiness," January 11, 2008, http://abcnews.go.com/Health/story?id=4115033.

5. Sonja Lyubomirsky, Kennon M. Sheldon, and David Schkade, "Pursuing Happiness: The Architecture of Sustainable Change," *Review of General Psychology* 9(2) (2005): 111–31.

6. "Effects on Attitudes," *Media Literary Council,* 2015, http://www.media literacycouncil.sg/media-issues/Pages/effects-on-attitudes.aspx#sthash .oG47TSPC.dpuf.

7. H. J. Garbán, F. J. Iribarren, and C. A. Noriega, "Using Biological Markers to Measure Stress in Listeners of Commercial Talk Radio," Chicano Studies Research Center Working Paper No. 3, *National Hispanic Media Coalition,* August 2012, http://www.nhmc.org/nhmcnew/wp-content/uploads/2013/03/RR_Hate Speech3.pdf.

8. Wendy M. Johnston and Graham C. L. Davey, "The Psychological Impact of Negative TV News Bulletins: The Catastrophizing of Personal Worries," *British Journal of Psychology* 88(pt.1) (February 1997): 85–91.

9. Guy Winch, "Why We All Need to Practice Emotional First Aid," *TED Talks,* November 2014, https://www.ted.com/talks/guy_winch_the_case_for _emotional_hygiene.

10. Carol Dweck, "The Power of Believing That You Can Improve," *TED*

Talks, November 2014, https://www.ted.com/talks/carol_dweck_the_power _of_believing_that_you_can_improve.

11. Carol Dweck, "How Can You Change from a Fixed Mindset to a Growth Mindset?" *Mindset,* http://mindsetonline.com/changeyourmindset/firststeps/.

12. 1 Corinthians 15:33.

13. Nicholas A. Christakis and James H. Fowler, "Friendship and Natural Selection," In the Light of Evolution VIII: Darwinian Thinking in the Social Sciences, *Proceedings of the National Academy of Sciences* 111 (Suppl 3) (July 22, 2014): 10796–801.

14. Inga Kiderra, "Friends Are the Family You Choose: Genome-Wide Analysis Reveals Genetic Similarities Among Friends," *UC San Diego News,* July 14, 2014, http://ucsdnews.ucsd.edu/pressrelease/friends_are_the_family_you_choose.

Connection

1. Barbara L. Fredrickson, "The Science of Love," *Aeon,* March 15, 2013, http://aeon.co/magazine/psychology/barbara-fredrickson-biology-of-love/.

2. Gallup Institute, "State of the American Workplace," 2013, http://employee engagement.com/wp-content/uploads/2013/06/Gallup-2013-State-of-the -American-Workplace-Report.pdf; Christine M. Riordan and Rodger W. Griffeth, "The Opportunity for Friendship in the Workplace: An Underexplored Construct," *Journal of Business and Psychology* 10(2) (December 1995): 141–54.

3. Tony Hsieh, *Delivering Happiness: A Path to Profits, Passion, and Purpose* (New York: Business Plus, 2010).

4. Gallup Institute, "State of the American Workplace."

5. Janice Kaplan, report on the Gratitude Survey conducted for the John Templeton Foundation, June–October 2012, in Emiliana R. Simon-Thomas and Jeremy Adam Smith, "How Grateful Are Americans?" January 10, 2013, http:// greatergood.berkeley.edu/article/item/how_grateful_are_americans.

6. Tony Isaacs, "Love, Romance and Travel Can Be Keys to Health and Longevity," *Natural News,* August 4, 2012, http://www.naturalnews.com/036686 _romance_health_longevity.html.

7. George Vaillant, *Triumphs of Experience: The Men of the Harvard Grant Study* (Cambridge, MA: Harvard Univ. Press, 2012).

8. Fredrickson, "Science of Love."

9. Fredrickson, "Science of Love."

10. Fredrickson, "Science of Love."

11. Proverbs 21:9.

12. Howard Friedman and Leslie Martin, *The Longevity Project: Surprising Discoveries for Health and Long Life from the Landmark Eight-Decade Study* (New York: Hudson Street, 2011).

13. Barbara L. Fredrickson, "Your Phone vs. Your Heart," *New York Times*, March 23, 2013, http://www.nytimes.com/2013/03/24/opinion/sunday/your-phone-vs-your-heart.html.

14. Shawn Achor, "Positive Intelligence," *Harvard Business Review*, January–February 2012, https://hbr.org/2012/01/positive-intelligence/ar/1.

15. Achor, "Positive Intelligence."

16. Dan Buettner, *The Blue Zones: Lessons for Living Longer from the People Who've Lived the Longest* (Washington, DC: National Geographic Society, 2008).

17. M. S. Hill, "Marital Stability and Spouses' Shared Time: A Multidisciplinary Hypothesis," *Journal of Family Issues* 9(4) (1988): 427–51.

18. B. Fraley and A. Aron, "The Effect of Shared Humorous Experience on Closeness in Initial Encounters," *Personal Relationships* 11(1) (2004): 61–78.

Meaning

1. Michael Steger, "Meaningful Living," http://www.michaelfsteger.com/?page_id=113.

2. Patricia Boyle et al., "Effect of Purpose in Life on the Relation Between Alzheimer Disease Pathologic Changes on Cognitive Function in Advanced Age," *Archives of General Psychiatry* 69(5) (May 2012): 499–504.

3. Earl Nightingale, "The Strangest Secret," *Nightingale Conant,* http://www.nightingale.com/articles/the-strangest-secret/.

4. Michael Steger, "What Makes Life Meaningful: Michael Steger at TEDxCSU," https://www.youtube.com/watch?v=RLFVoEF2RIo.

5. "Having a Sense of Purpose May Add Years to Your Life," *Psychological Science,* May 12, 2014, http://www.psychologicalscience.org/index.php/news/releases/having-a-sense-of-purpose-in-life-may-add-years-to-your-life.html; Patrick Hill and Nicholas Turiano, "Purpose in Life as a Predictor of Mortality Across Adulthood," *Psychological Science,* May 8, 2014, doi:10.1177/09567976 1431799.

6. Mount Sinai Medical Center, "Have a Sense of Purpose in Life? It May

Protect Your Heart," *Science Daily,* March 6, 2015, http://www.sciencedaily.com/releases/2015/03/150306132538.htm.

7. Boyle et al., "Effect of Purpose in Life."

8. Sharon Salzberg, *Real Happiness at Work: Meditations for Accomplishment, Achievement, and Peace* (New York: Workman, 2014).

9. Roy Baumeister, "The Meanings of Life," Aeon.co, September 16, 2013, http://aeon.co/magazine/psychology/do-you-want-a-meaningful-life-or-a-happy-one/.

Creativity

1. Dictionary.com, s.v. "creativity," http://dictionary.reference.com/browse/creativity?s=t.

2. Shelley Carson, *Your Creative Brain: Seven Steps to Maximize Imagination, Productivity and Innovation in Your Life* (San Francisco: Jossey-Bass, 2010).

3. Mihaly Csikszentmihalyi, *Flow: The Psychology of Optimal Experience* (New York: Harper and Row, 1990).

4. Steven Kotler, *The Rise of Superman: Decoding the Science of Ultimate Human Performance* (New York: Houghton Mifflin Harcourt, 2014).

5. Scott Barry Kaufman, "The Real Neuroscience of Creativity," *Scientific American,* August 19, 2013, http://blogs.scientificamerican.com/beautiful-minds/the-real-neuroscience-of-creativity/.

6. Julia Cameron, *The Artist's Way: A Spiritual Path to Higher Creativity* (New York: Tarcher/Putnam, 1992).

7. April Armstrong, "Happy Emotions Boost Creativity," *ABC News,* December 19, 2006, http://abcnews.go.com/Health/story?id=2736053.

8. Carrie Barron and Alton Barron, *The Creativity Cure: How to Build Happiness with Your Own Two Hands* (New York: Scribner, 2012).

9. Paul J. Silvia et al., "Everyday Creativity in Daily Life: An Experience-Sampling Study of 'Little c' Creativity," *Psychology of Aesthetics, Creativity, and the Arts* 8(2) (May 2014): 183–88.

10. Stuart Brown, *Play: How It Shapes the Brain, Opens the Imagination and Invigorates the Soul* (New York: Avery, 2009).

11. "State of Create Study," *Adobe,* April 2012, http://www.adobe.com/aboutadobe/pressroom/pdfs/Adobe_State_of_Create_Global_Benchmark_Study.pdf.

12. Some of the research for the "Start Playing!" section was collected and written about by Live Happy editor Chris Libby in "It's OK to Play," *Live Happy*, October 2014, 81–82.

13. Rebecca L. McMillan, Scott Barry Kaufman, and Jerome L. Singer, "Ode to Positive Constructive Daydreaming," *Frontiers in Psychology*, September 23, 2013, http://journal.frontiersin.org/article/10.3389/fpsyg.2013.00626/full.

14. Daniel J. Levitin, *This Is Your Brain on Music: The Science of a Human Obsession* (New York: Plume, 2006).

Gratitude

1. Sonja Lyubomirsky, *The How of Happiness: A New Approach to Getting the Life You Want* (New York: Penguin, 2007).

2. Robert A. Emmons, "The Benefits of Gratitude," *Greater Good*, November 2010, http://greatergood.berkeley.edu/gg_live/science_meaningful_life_videos/speaker/robert_emmons/the_benefits_of_gratitude/.

3. Robert A. Emmons and Michael McCullough, "Counting Blessings Versus Burdens: An Experimental Investigation of Gratitude and Subjective Well-Being in Daily Life," *Journal of Personality and Social Psychology* 84(2) (February 2003): 377–89, http://greatergood.berkeley.edu/pdfs/GratitudePDFs/6Emmons-BlessingsBurdens.pdf.

4. Alex Korb, "The Grateful Brain," *Psychology Today*, November 20, 2012, https://www.psychologytoday.com/blog/prefrontal-nudity/201211/the-grateful-brain.

5. Much of the research cited in this chapter was collected and reported by Live Happy science editor Paula Felps in her article "Brain Matters: Mindfulness Can Change the Way You Think, How You Feel," *Live Happy*.

6. Barbara L. Fredrickson et al., "What Good Are Positive Emotions in Crisis? A Prospective Study of Resilience and Emotions Following the Terrorist Attacks on the United States on September 11th, 2001," *Journal of Personality and Social Psychology* 84(2) (February 2003): 365–76; Todd B. Kashdan, Gitendra Uswatte and Terri Julian, "Gratitude and Hedonic and Eudaimonic Well-Being in Vietnam War Veterans," *Behaviour Research and Therapy*, 44(2) (February 2006): 177–99.

7. Sara B. Algoe, Shelly L. Gable, and Natalya C. Maisel, "It's the Little Things: Everyday Gratitude as a Booster Shot for Romantic Relationships,"

Personal Relationships 17 (2010): 217–33, http://greatergood.berkeley.edu/images/application_uploads/Algoe-GratitudeAndRomance.pdf.

8. Janice Kaplan, report on the Gratitude Survey conducted for the John Templeton Foundation, June–October 2012, in Emiliana R. Simon-Thomas and Jeremy Adam Smith, "How Grateful Are Americans?" January 10, 2013, http://greatergood.berkeley.edu/article/item/how_grateful_are_americans.

9. Felps, "Brain Matters."

10. Robert A. Emmons, "10 Ways to Become More Grateful," November 17, 2010, http://greatergood.berkeley.edu/article/item/ten_ways_to_become_more_grateful1/.

Mindfulness

1. Felps, "Brain Matters."

2. Maia Szalavitz, "Q & A: Jon Kabat-Zinn Talks About Bringing Mindfulness Meditation to Medicine," *Time,* January 11, 2012, http://healthland.time.com/2012/01/11/mind-reading-jon-kabat-zinn-talks-about-bringing-mindfulness-meditation-to-medicine/.

3. Much of the research cited in this chapter was collected and reported by Live Happy science editor Paula Felps in her article "Give Yourself a Mindfulness Makeover," *Live Happy,* August 21, 2015, http://www.livehappy.com/practice/give-yourself-mindfulness-makeover.

Health

1. Dan Buettner, *The Blue Zones: Lessons for Living Longer from the People Who've Lived the Longest* (Washington, DC: National Geographic Society, 2008).

2. Kara Swisher, "AOL Has Been in Talks to Spin Off HuffPost as Part of Verizon Acquisition Deal," *Re/code,* May 12, 2015, http://recode.net/2015/05/12/aol-in-talks-to-spin-off-huffpost-as-part-of-acquisition-deal/.

3. Paul D. Loprinzi and Bradley J. Cardinal, "Association Between Objectively-Measured Physical Activity and Sleep NHANES 2005–2006," 4(2) (December 2011): 65–69, http://www.sciencedirect.com/science/article/pii/S1755296611000317.

4. "Working Out May Help Prevent Colds, Flu," *NBC News,* January 17, 2006, http://www.nbcnews.com/id/10894093/ns/health-cold_and_flu/t/working-out-may-help-prevent-colds-flu/#.T2vztWJAaOF.

5. Chi Pang Wen et al., "Minimum Amount of Physical Activity for Reduced Mortality and Extended Life Expectancy: A Prospective Cohort Study," *Lancet* 378(9798) (October 1, 2011): 1244–53, http://www.thelancet.com/journals/lancet/article/PIIS0140-6736(11)60749-6/abstract.

6. Michelle Segar, *No Sweat: How the Simple Science of Motivation Can Bring You a Lifetime of Fitness* (New York: Amacom, 2015).

7. John Ratey, *Spark: The Revolutionary New Science of Exercise and the Brain* (New York: Little, Brown, 2008).

8. Paula Felps, "The Science of Happy Foods," *Live Happy* magazine, June 2014.

9. Felice N. Jacka et al., "Association of Western and Traditional Diets with Depression and Anxiety in Women," *The American Journal of Psychiatry* 167(3) (March 2010): 305–11.

10. Tasnime N. Akbaraly, et al., "Dietary Pattern and Depressive Symptoms in Middle Age," *The British Journal of Psychiatry* 195(5) (October 2009): 408–13.

11. Felps, "The Science of Happy Foods."

Resilience

1. George S. Everly Jr., Douglas A. Strouse, and Dennis K. McCormack, *Stronger: Develop the Resilience You Need to Succeed* (New York: Amacom, 2015).

2. Bonnie Benard, *Fostering Resilience in Children* (Urbana, IL: ERIC Clearinghouse on Elementary and Early Childhood Education, 1995 [ED386327]), http://www.edpsycinteractive.org/files/resilience.html.

3. Ryan Santos, "Why Resilience? A Review of Literature of Resilience and Implications for Further Educational Research," dissertation, Claremont Graduate University and San Diego State University Joint Ph.D. Program in Education, http://go.sdsu.edu/education/doc/files/01370-ResiliencyLiteratureReview (SDSU).pdf.

4. Research and portions of this chapter were taken from Janice Arenofsky, "The Bounce-Back Effect," *Live Happy,* June 2015, http://www.livehappy.com/self/resilience/bounce-back-effect.

Spirituality

1. Christopher Peterson and Martin Seligman, *Character Strengths and Virtues: A Handbook and Classification* (Washington, DC: American Psychological Association; New York: Oxford Univ. Press, 2004), 601.

2. "Spirituality Is Key to Kids' Happiness, Study Suggests," *ScienceDaily,* January 12, 2009, http://www.sciencedaily.com/releases/2009/01/090108082904.htm.

3. Rebecca Gladding, "This Is Your Brain on Meditation," *Psychology Today,* May 22, 2013, https://www.psychologytoday.com/blog/use-your-mind-change-your-brain/201305/is-your-brain-meditation.

4. C. G. Ellison, "Religious Involvement and Subjective Well-being," *Journal of Health and Social Behavior* 32(1) (March 1991): 80–99.

5. Raphael Bonelli et al., "Religious and Spiritual Factors in Depression: Review and Integration of the Research," *Depression Research and Treatment* 2012 (2012): 1–9.

6. Itai Ivtzan et al., "Well-being Through Self-Fulfillment: Examining Developmental Aspects of Self-Actualization," *Humanistic Psychologist* 41(2) (April 2013): 119–32.

7. Robert A. Hummer et al., "Religious Involvement and U.S. Adult Mortality," *Demography* 36(2) (May 1999): 273–85.

8. Peterson and Seligman, *Character Strengths and Virtues.*

9. Chaeyoon Lima and Robert D. Putnam, "Religion, Social Networks, and Life Satisfaction," *American Sociological Review* 75(6) (2010): 914–33, http://wcfia.harvard.edu/files/wcfia/files/rputnam_religion_social_networks.pdf.

10. Janice Kaplan, report on the Gratitude Survey conducted for the John Templeton Foundation, June–October 2012, in Emiliana R. Simon-Thomas and Jeremy Adam Smith, "How Grateful Are Americans?" January 10, 2013, http://greatergood.berkeley.edu/article/item/how_grateful_are_americans.

11. H. G. Koenig, D. E. King, and V. B. Carson, *Handbook of Religion and Health,* 2nd ed. (New York: Oxford Univ. Press, 2012), cited in Bonelli et al., "Religious and Spiritual Factors in Depression," 4.

12. Elisha Goldstein, "Cultivating the Sacred in Your Life," *ElishaGoldstein.com,* February 13, 2012, http://elishagoldstein.com/blog/2012/02/cultivating-the-sacred-in-your-life/.

Giving Back

1. Melanie Rudd, Jennifer Aaker, and Michael I. Norton, "Leave Them Smiling: How Small Acts Create More Happiness Than Large Acts," December 16, 2011, http://faculty-gsb.stanford.edu/aaker/pages/documents/LeaveThemSmiling_RuddAakerNorton12-16-11.pdf.

2. Rodlescia S. Sneed and Sheldon Cohen, "A Prospective Study of Volunteerism and Hypertension Risk in Older Adults," *Psychology and Aging* 28(2) (June 2013): 578–86.

3. R. Grimm, K. Spring, and N. Dietz, *The Health Benefits of Volunteering: A Review of Recent Research* (Washington, DC: Corporation for National and Community Service, Office of Research and Policy, 2007).

4. Grimm, Spring, and Dietz, *The Health Benefits of Volunteering*.

5. James H. Fowler and Nicholas A. Christakis, "Cooperative Behavior Cascades in Human Social Networks," *Proceedings of the National Academy of Sciences* 107(12) (2010): 5334–38.